I0211898

Animal Writes

Prompts and Practices to Guide the Animal Writer's Journey

Published by Ashland Creek Press in Ashland, Oregon

www.ashlandcreekpress.com

© 2025 Midge Raymond & John Yunker

ISBN 978-1-61822-103-2

Library of Congress Cataloging-in-Publication Data

Names: Raymond, Midge, author. | Yunker, John, author.
Title: Animal writes : prompts and practices to guide the animal writer's journey / Midge Raymond & John Yunker.
Description: Ashland, Oregon : Ashland Creek Press, 2025. | Summary: "Animal Writes is for the animal lover who craves insights and inspiration for taking their passion through to publication. The book includes lessons learned from a decade of writing and teaching writing -- as well as writing prompts to inspire your writing -- fiction, nonfiction or poetry"-- Provided by publisher.
Identifiers: LCCN 2024057704 (print) | LCCN 2024057705 (ebook) | ISBN 9781618221032 (paperback) | ISBN 9781618221049 (epub)
Subjects: LCSH: Creative writing. | Animals in literature. | Animal welfare in literature.
Classification: LCC PN171.A55 .R39 2025 (print) | LCC PN171.A55 (ebook) | DDC 808.02--dc23/eng/20250204
LC record available at https://lccn.loc.gov/2024057704
LC ebook record available at https://lccn.loc.gov/2024057705

Animal Writes

Prompts and Practices to Guide the
Animal Writer's Journey

Midge Raymond & John Yunker

Ashland
Creek
Press Est. 2011

"Making a living is nothing; the great
difficulty is making a point, making a
difference—with words."
—Elizabeth Hardwick

"There is nothing so powerful as an idea
whose time has come."
—Victor Hugo

"Until the lions have their historians, tales
of the hunt shall always glorify the hunter."
—African proverb

Contents

Part 4: Along the Way: Prompts & Inspiration

Part 5: Paths to Publication

Introduction

In 2018, we published *Writing for Animals*, a book that featured a range of inspiring and instructional essays about advocating for animals through your writing. The book led to a class of the same name. Throughout these classes, we met fellow writers from around the world, from poets to memoirists to novelists, some published and others just getting started. But what we all had in common was that we were each, in our own ways, on a journey.

Finding the journey that's right for you

This book distills lessons from our classes, from our fellow writers, and from our experiences as writers and publishers of animal-centric literature. The book is intended to both guide and inspire you on your journey as a writer and animal advocate.

Along the way, we will highlight the many different genres that writers pursue when writing for animals as well as different approaches to publication.

Writing prompts to jump-start or refuel

Writing isn't easy. For every burst of creativity, a writer may suffer through droughts spent staring at blank pages. That's where the writing prompts fit in. Throughout this book you will find prompts to help you think differently, try on new points of view, and develop the voices of your nonhuman characters.

Writing is a journey without end. And keep in mind that the journey you take should and will be your own unique path.

While we can shine a light on common ways forward, you may discover a new path that has not yet been taken. Regardless of where you go, our hope is that this book becomes a trusted companion along the way.

—Midge & John

Part 1:
Preparation

Why write for animals?

Why are you writing for animals?

Perhaps it is to portray an animal in your life. Or perhaps it is to shine a light on a species that is overlooked or, worse, villainized. Perhaps you write to explore animals you've never seen in person. Or perhaps you simply have a passion for sharing your love of animals.

Knowing *why* you are writing for animals is as important as the writing itself.

Because the *why* is what will propel you on your journey and keep you going along the way. The life of a writer can be challenging in the best of times—but writing for animals can be doubly so, particularly if you're writing to protect or save a species that society cares little about.

Our journey began more than a decade ago when we came to realize, as writers, how seldom animals are portrayed accurately, wisely, or compassionately in literature. And that even most writers who love animals continue to eat, wear, and use them.

Animals are sentient beings who deserve freedom and protection—yet while activists know this, and science is beginning to learn how smart and emotional animals are, our literature still has a long way to go. Although seeing overt animal abuse in fiction isn't necessarily common, such actions as eating or wearing animals and going to zoos or circuses or the horse races are very common—and aren't considered abusive at all, despite the necessary violence that is done to animals in these situations.

As both vegans and writers, we want to create a better world for animals. Being vegan is the easy part—but as writers, we know we can do more. If we want to see a better future for all living creatures, we need to start by imagining it. And what better place to do this than in stories?

What's often missing in literature is the idea of animals as individuals, as characters in their own right. All too often, animals are deployed as props. For example, a swimmer in the ocean may encounter a shark, simply as a means of heightening tension—despite the fact that a swimmer is far more likely to die by drowning than by shark attack. These long-accepted tropes are overdue to be questioned and challenged. Writers have the power to educate readers while simultaneously entertaining them.

Another reason we believe in creative writing about animals is that fiction reaches us in places facts cannot. Readers who don't want to learn about endangered species—or who may feel too depressed or overwhelmed by reading a whole book on the topic—may be totally open to reading a thriller or a romance or a literary novel in which an endangered species is featured. Best of all, they'll be engaged in a story while learning something new, and perhaps even opening their minds and hearts to a species they hadn't considered before.

Advocating for animals is more important than ever, not just because of climate change but because of the unsustainability of human population growth, which increases the toll on animals as well as the planet—animals everywhere are losing their habitats due to increased demands for agriculture as well as housing and development.

When it comes to animal rights, the animals cannot have too many supporters. You may be a vegan activist, or you may be an omnivorous writer who wants to write about animals in your creative work. *Animal Writes* is for all advocates, and for all writers. The aim of this book is to encourage you to explore your relationship with animals, both on and off the page, and to incorporate as much compassion as possible into your writing—which will enhance your creativity as well as help create a better world for animals.

This book is about writing *for* animals rather than merely writing *about* them. It's about asking what we as humans can do for animals rather than what they can do for us. It's about listening to them and to our hearts. Most of all, it's about putting pen to paper.

Your own relationship with animals—then and now

Some of us have seen animals as sentient beings since childhood; some of us were raised vegetarian, or even vegan. Most of us, however, come to this awakening later in life: that all animals are created equal, that there is no difference between a dog and a pig, and therefore no good or humane reason that dogs are legally protected from abuse while the abuse and slaughter of pigs is lawful. And for most of us, it's a tough awakening, especially if we've eaten or worn animals for most of our lives, or if we've used them for entertainment or other purposes.

This book is not only for vegetarians or vegans—some of you may still be on this journey; perhaps you're eating less meat or phasing out leather. For every human who goes vegan overnight, there are others who take a longer road. We respect everyone who is on that journey, wherever they may be, as it's not an easy road to travel. But it's a journey well worth taking. It's never too late to change and evolve—and to help others do the same, through our writing.

Animals need supporters from every walk of life, and this book is about literary activism: using your talents as a writer to advocate for animals, whether it's through journalism, through poetry or fiction, through memoir, or by telling animals' stories on social media.

✎ WRITING PROMPT

- Write about your family's attitude toward animals, from pets to food, when you were growing up.
- What is different for you today, if anything, from how you were raised to view animals?
- How would you like your own life to evolve in terms of how you see animals?

✎ WRITING PROMPT

- Write about your favorite animal as a child.
- Write about your favorite animal now, as an adult.
- If your favorite animal is different, how and why do you think this shifted for you?
- What animal(s) do you imagine appreciating more in the future than you do now?

Writing *for* animals

Peter Benchley came to regret his portrayal of sharks in his bestseller *Jaws*, which created false perceptions of sharks and unwarranted fears. Benchley later became an advocate for shark conservation—yet how much better might sharks have fared if this novel hadn't ignited so much misguided fear in its readers?

> What I now know, which wasn't known when I wrote *Jaws*, is that there is no such thing as a rogue shark which develops a taste for human flesh. No one appreciates how vulnerable they are to destruction.
> —Peter Benchley

One aspect of writing *for* animals rather than simply *about* animals is creating work that has the potential to improve the lives of animals, rather than portraying animals in ways that are solely in service to the human characters. Most of all, writers have tremendous power as creators and must use this power wisely and for good. Always be aware of how your story might adversely affect the lives of animals.

✐ WRITING PROMPT

- Write about a book, article, etc. that you felt did a disservice to an animal.

- What were the elements of the piece (such as language, focus, information or lack thereof) that made you feel this way?

One thing to keep in mind as we write about animals is that we're artists, not scientists. You'll learn more later in this book about the importance of research (and *Jaws* is a cautionary tale of writing about animals without knowing them well), but do keep in mind that you're not writing creatively in order to prepare students for a biology exam. You're writing to tell a story. So do feel free to take creative license—such as writing speculative fiction, or writing from an animal's point of view—but be sure to do it thoughtfully and authentically.

As writers and publishers of animal-themed fiction, we've seen firsthand that the world is not quite ready to see animals as anywhere near equal to humans. We've also seen, in the last decade-plus since founding Ashland Creek Press, that the world is evolving. We're seeing more books about animals being published by mainstream publishers—not just animal memoirs but books like Deb Olin Unferth's *Barn 8*, a novel about chicken farming—and we're seeing reviewers and readers embrace such books.

So while you may feel as though you're the only one who is writing about animals, you're far from alone. And you may notice that your animal-themed stories are harder to publish—and we tackle this later in the book as well—but know that this won't last forever. Remember that any worthwhile advocacy is first met with resistance, and this includes writing for animals. The important thing is to keep going.

✐ WRITING PROMPT

- Write about a time you saw someone treat an animal in a way you didn't like.

- What did you do (or not do) when you witnessed this?

- What was the outcome (for you/the other person/ the animal)?

- How did this change how you view animals and how they are treated?

✐ WRITING PROMPT

- Write about an animal you're afraid of.

- Where did this fear originate? Is it based on reality, or a misperception?

- Write about an affectionate encounter (real or fictional) with the animal you fear.

✐ WRITING PROMPT

- Write about an animal that doesn't exist (to our knowledge) but that you wish did (as one example, a lot of Pacific Northwesterners believe in Sasquatch).

- Write a scene that features this animal ...
    - in a lab
    - in their natural habitat
    - as a pet

Sad stories about animals (who are more often than not victimized by humans) are too numerous (and too heartbreaking) to count. Yet this is why we write about animals—to change their lives for the better.

The following prompts will not be easy to write, but they are helpful for anyone who writes about animals. We need to go to these tragic places in order to understand what's at stake for each individual. Even if graphic or unsettling details don't make it into your final draft, it's important to experience these things on the page so that you're writing from a place of authenticity. Note: If you don't have enough firsthand knowledge of any of these prompts, do some research before writing.

✎ WRITING PROMPT

- Write from the point of view of one of these animals.

    ° A cat whose owner has died and finds himself in a shelter.

    ° A dog who is kept chained outside all day long.

    ° A seal who starves because his belly is filled with plastics.

    ° An African elephant who is killed by poachers for her tusks. (Don't neglect to consider her family.)

    ° A cow whose baby is taken from her because her milk will go to humans. (She can live on a large factory farm or a small dairy.)

    ° A fluffy male chick who is put into a grinder because he will never lay eggs and therefore is considered "useless."

Discovering your activist style

You may not think of yourself as an activist, but you probably are in your own way. If you've ever written a letter to the editor, you're an activist. If you've ever stood up for someone (human or nonhuman) who needed an ally, you're an activist. Not all activists march on Washington or occupy Wall Street or hold signs outside courtrooms or restaurants or slaughterhouses.

As writers, we're introverts—and because of this we consider ourselves literary activists. We write about animals from the perspective of helping them, and at Ashland Creek Press, we publish writers who ask their readers—through books in all genres, including essays, short stories, young adult fiction, thrillers, romantic comedies, and literary fiction—to take a closer look at their own relationships to animals.

When we volunteered with the Center for Ecosystem Sentinels years ago, helping with a penguin census, we both were so incredibly inspired by the dedication of the researchers to a species that desperately needs attention (and science that needs funding). While it wasn't in the cards for us to become conservation biologists and undertake the same work, we could certainly bring readers into this world and show them the work being done, and why it needs to be done. John's novel *The Tourist Trail* is a thriller that takes readers from a penguin colony in Argentina to a ship of anti-whaling activists (along with an undercover FBI agent and a whirlwind romance). Midge's novel *My Last Continent* is a more literary novel about a penguin researcher in the Antarctic who finally finds love with a fellow researcher, only to face losing everything when a ship sinks in the Southern Ocean. Perhaps the best thing about being a writer is that you don't have to limit yourself to any one thing—we can help animals in any number of ways, by living and researching and following our passions and, most of all, by writing.

✎ WRITING PROMPT

- Write about someone who inspires you. This person doesn't have to be an animal advocate, just someone whose passion you connect with.

- What about this person do you admire?

- How does this person inspire or attract others?

- In what ways can you turn your own love of animals into advocacy?

✎ WRITING PROMPT

- Think of a job or career you'd like to have, if you could.

- What about this work are you drawn to?

- In what ways could you change the world for animals in this career?

✎ WRITING PROMPT

- Milan Kundera described characters as "experimental selves." Write a scene for each of the following scenarios in which you are the main character, drawing upon both your own character traits as well as any "experimental selves" that are within you …

- ° Marching for animal rights
- ° Writing a letter to the editor to protect a species
- ° Rescuing an animal from a factory farm
- ° Caring for animals at a sanctuary
- ° Saving a companion animal from abuse
- ° Taking in a stray
- ° Protesting a restaurant that serves foie gras
- ° Advocating to protect an animal's habitat
- ° Studying an endangered species
- ° Doing a tree sit to protect a forest
- ° Protesting hunting or fishing for sport

Discovering your writing style

You may already be a fiction writer or a journalist, a poet or an essayist—but even if you know your genre, you may find that as you write about animals, you might branch out into another genre or two. This section, tailored for those who are new to creative writing and/or publishing their work, offers a brief overview of genres and styles.

Nonfiction falls into the areas of narrative nonfiction—such as long-form journalism, articles, and op-eds—and creative nonfiction, such as memoir or essays. Anything labeled nonfiction is a true story, though in memoir and essay, some creative license is to be expected.

Fiction refers to stories that are created, as in novels and short stories. Poetry tells stories that are both true and imagined.

If you've finished a piece and aren't sure where it falls on the fictional spectrum, below are approximate word and page counts for works of fiction (note that the "rules" are similar for essays and short stories, and for memoirs and novels).

Short story

- 1,000 to 10,000 words
- 4 to 40 pages

Examples:
- Ernest Hemingway, "Hills Like White Elephants" (1,600 words)

- Annie Proulx, "Brokeback Mountain" (10,000 words)

Flash fiction

- 5 to 1,000 words

Examples:

- Joyce Carol Oates, "Widow's First Year" (4 words)
- Amy Hempel, "Memoir" (17 words)
- Jamaica Kincaid, "Girl" (685 words)

Novella

- 20,000 to 40,000 words
- 80 to 160 pages

Examples:

- Stephen King, *Different Seasons*, an anthology of four novellas (500 pages total)
- Lan Samantha Chang, *Hunger*, a novella and stories (191 pages total)
- Joseph Conrad, *Heart of Darkness* (80 pages)
- Sandra Cisneros, *The House on Mango Street* (105 pages)

Novel

- 60,000+ words

- 240+ pages

Examples:
- Jerzy Kosiński, *Being There* (128 pages)
- Leo Tolstoy, *War and Peace* (1,400 pages)

✎ WRITING PROMPT
- What is your favorite genre to read?
- In what genre do you usually write?
- Do your reading/writing interests align?
- If so, in what ways? If not, how might you align them?

✎ WRITING PROMPT
- Take a work that you have completed and write it in a different genre. For example …
  - ° Turn an essay into a fictional short story.
  - ° Turn a poem into an essay or story.
  - ° Distill your novel or memoir into a poem.

Part 2:
Language Matters

Your journey through language

Words are the tools we use to change the world. And words carry historical, cultural, and emotional baggage. Every word you use should be used intentionally, and sometimes this intentionality comes only in the second, third, or fourth revision.

When writing about animals, we enter a world of language that reflects thousands of years of viewing animals as enemies or property or products. *Livestock*, for example, refers to animals raised for consumption. Yet a writer who wants to encourage readers to see cows or sheep in a new light would avoid this word, as it has abstracted animals, thereby abstracting any emotional connection one might feel.

As you embark on your writing journey, we want you to consider every word you use, read, see, and hear. This chapter includes a collection of phrases that we often hear but don't have to repeat (at least not unintentionally). We also include esoterica around describing animals, in youth and in groups.

Rethinking our language

We've all grown up with sayings that involve animals—such as *kill two birds with one stone*—and, like many other habits, ceasing to use these phrases can be a challenge if we've used them without thinking for most of our lives.

Yet language does matter, and rethinking how we speak and write is essential to advocating for animals. We can hardly be literary activists when saying such things as, "Sure, I'll be your guinea pig for this new recipe."

Activists are already tackling this issue in myriad ways. As one example, during the 2021 World Series, PETA proposed that Major League Baseball do away with the word *bullpen*—which refers to the holding area where terrified bulls are kept before slaughter—in favor of an updated, more animal-friendly term. In its press release, PETA's executive vice president Tracy Reiman states, "Words matter, and baseball 'bullpens' devalue talented players and mock the misery of sensitive animals ... PETA encourages Major League Baseball coaches, announcers, players, and fans to *changeup* [*sic*] their language and embrace the 'arm barn' instead."

And changing our language is not just for idioms—an encouraging 2021 *New York Times* headline read, "Don't Call Them 'Shark Attacks,' Scientists Say," referring to *The Sydney Morning Herald*'s decision to replace the word *attack* with such terms as *bites*, *incidents*, and *encounters*. With the shark populations having decreased more than 70 percent since 1970, the article notes, scientists hope that less sensational language will change the public's view of these animals who, in fact, do not attack but are provoked by humans who get too close, step on them, or are mistaken for seals. And another fact is that shark-human incidents remain extremely rare.

Changes are being encouraged in scientific circles as well. In their article "Caring, killing, euphemism and George Orwell: How language choice undercuts our mission" in *Biological Conservation* (2017, vol. 211), authors David Johns and Dominick A. DellaSala write about Orwell's understanding of the power of language as they argue that conservation biologists should avoid euphemism as "a means to mask the indefensible." The use of euphemism, they write, compromises the efforts of conservation biology to inspire us to care for the planet, and euphemistic language is both distancing and misleading. They suggest being more direct—instead of writing "we harvested a sample of 100 fish," to write, "we caught and killed 100 fish." This may not be pretty language, but it is honest and real.

And if you ever wonder whether you're inadvertently using euphemistic language, Johns and DellaSala offer a self-test: "Apply the term or phrase to some entity or group you care about and gauge your reaction. If you are uncomfortable it is probably a euphemism. If it makes you feel dishonest it almost certainly is a euphemism. Would you 'sacrifice' or 'cull' those you care about so that some knowledge might be gained?"

As readers skim over innocuous words like *cull, harvest,* and *take,* they remain removed from reality—and this is the way certain industries like it, so we will not think of the cruelty to our planet and its animals. What's so sneaky about language in this sense is that it can be used to perpetuate cruelty, and this is exactly what it does.

The author and activist Brigid Brophy puts it another way: "Whenever people say, 'We mustn't be sentimental,' you can take it they are about to do something cruel. And if they add, 'We must be realistic,' they mean they are going to make money out of it."

The good news about this is that language can also be used to clarify. As writers and activists, we have the power—and the obligation—to change our language so that it tells the truth rather than obfuscates it. Once we begin using words that show the reality of how we treat animals, we will be on a path to stop using and abusing them.

New words for old ideas

Below are some examples—and you surely know of many more—of idioms involving animals, their traditional meanings, and how we might phrase them differently. Rethinking language can be challenging, especially among those who don't revere animals as much as we literary activists do, and so we encourage a simple route. Humor can work, too—such as replacing the phrase *kill two birds with one stone* with something like *kill two bagels with one scone* (yes, we've actually heard this one, and we actually sort of like it)—though only if you want to draw attention to the issue. Which, in certain situations, can be a very good thing.

Note that some of these examples refer to horrific practices— dog racing, animal testing—and that others are pretty innocuous, such as *being a night owl*. We wanted to offer a few of the most egregious idioms—those that refer to animal abuse—in hopes of seeing these disappear from our everyday talk, but we included a few more just to show how prevalent this language is. *Being a night owl*, for example, isn't disparaging owls—it is, in fact, acknowledging how they live their lives, and comparing oneself to an owl could even be considered a compliment. However, it's important to be aware of how and why we use idioms, and especially to do so in a way that doesn't perpetuate animal abuse in glib, offhand ways.

Speaking of compliments, many of these idioms are anything but. So, while we've provided alternatives to the saying *ridden hard and put away wet*, they're not exactly terrific substitutions in that they're still insults. But at least they don't also insult animals!

The final reason to avoid these sayings in your writing is that they are "tired" sayings—meaning they are overused, border on cliché, and don't add anything original to dialogue or narrative. (Also: See our exceptions to the rules, following this list.)

She's living "high on the hog."

Being wealthy or well off, alluding to the most expensive cuts of meat from a hog.

She's living large. She's living the high life.

I don't have "a dog in the race/a dog in the fight."

Having an interest in a situation and/or outcome, referring to gambling on dog racing and/or dog fighting.

I'm not invested in this. I don't mind either way.

My kids are "guinea pigs" for all my new recipes.

Being tested/experimented on for any new, untried thing, as guinea pigs have been used for many scientific experiments.

My kids are my taste testers. My kids provide early reviews of my recipes.

You look like you've been "ridden hard and put away wet."

Referring to someone who looks worn out, alluding to a horse who's been worked hard and returned to the stable without being allowed to cool down.

You look like shit. You look exhausted. Are you okay?

He's the "underdog" in this match.

Being unlikely to win or prevail, referring to the losing dog in a dogfight.

He's a long shot in this match. He doesn't stand a chance.

I've got "bigger fish to fry."

Having something better to do, referring to cooking a bigger fish being better than a smaller one.

I've got better things to do. I've got more important things to do.

He's such a "birdbrain."

Referring to someone who is dim-witted or unintelligent, apparently due to the misperception of birds being stupid; birds are, in fact, cognitively superior to most mammals.

He's not the brightest. He's a little slow.

I "smell a rat."

Referring to things that aren't what they seem to be, or accusing someone of being an informant.

I don't believe it. Something isn't quite right here. He/she/they aren't what you think.

Something's fishy about this.

Similar to "smelling a rat," this refers to something not being what it appears to be.

Something isn't quite right about this. Something's off.

It's like "shooting fish in a barrel."

Referring to the ease of something, akin to shooting fish that are trapped in a barrel.

It's like falling off a log. It's a walk in the park. It's a slam dunk.

She's always been a "night owl."

Referring to someone who stays up late, whose best hours are later in the day/night, like owls, who are nocturnal.

She's nocturnal. She likes working nights. She's a late riser.

From the top of the hill, you get a "bird's-eye view" of the city.

Referring to a wide, vast aerial view, as people might experience if they were a bird flying overhead.

You get an aerial view. You can see everything from there.

Exceptions to the rule: your fictional characters

While the enlightened characters in your stories may wisely sidestep these animal sayings, you may also have created characters who are far less enlightened. In this case, these sayings may be appropriate and would reveal character. Also, the use of these sayings by certain characters could create conflict with more enlightened characters. When writing fiction, always remember that words reflect the characters who speak them.

The esoterica of animal writing

Writing about animals well requires not only respect but authenticity. We include this section on animal terms just as a starting point; whatever the species you're writing about, be sure to research the animals exhaustively, getting all their stories.

If you're writing about pilot whales, for example, you would know that they are the only species, other than humans and orcas, to go through menopause. If you're writing about penguins, you'll know that despite their romantic image, they're not as monogamous as we think (they are known to divorce or leave their mates for someone with a better nest, and they'll often move on if a mate comes home too late). And those adorable meerkats we all know and love can be ruthlessly and violently competitive.

In other words, all animals live in their own very unique worlds, and it's our job as writers to know these worlds as well as our own. How else can we authentically portray them? We are fortunate to live in an era where information is a click away, but learning a species well requires going far beyond internet research. (Read on for more about the myriad types of research you can do to learn about animals, both in this section and in Part 3.)

Animal babies

This is by no means an exhaustive list, and we've left out a few better-known animals (dog babies being puppies is fairly common knowledge) in favor of some of the more unusual animals whose baby names are often surprising.

- Aardvark: cub
- Albatross: chick
- Alligator: hatchling
- Ant: larva, pupa
- Anteater: pup
- Antelope: calf
- Ape: baby, child, infant
- Baboon: infant
- Badger: cub, kit
- Bat: pup
- Bear: cub
- Beaver: kit, kitten, pup
- Bee: larva, pupa
- Bobcat: bobkitten
- Buffalo: calf
- Camel: calf
- Chimpanzee: infant
- Cockroach: nymph
- Cormorant: chick, shaglet
- Coyote: cub, pup, puppy, whelp
- Cricket: nymph

- Crocodile: hatchling
- Deer: calf, fawn
- Dolphin: calf
- Donkey: foal
- Dragonfly: nymph
- Duck: duckling
- Eagle: eaglet, fledgling
- Elephant: calf
- Fish: fingerling, fry
- Fox: cub, kit, pup
- Gerbil: pup
- Giraffe: calf
- Goat: kid
- Goose: gosling
- Gorilla: infant
- Grasshopper: nymph
- Hamster: pup
- Hawk: eyas
- Hedgehog: hoglet, piglet, pup
- Horse: colt (male), filly (female), foal, weanling, yearling
- Hyena: cub
- Jaguar: cub
- Jellyfish: ephyra, planula, polyp
- Kangaroo: joey
- Lizard: hatchling

- Meerkat: meerkitten
- Mole: pup
- Mosquito: nymph, tumbler
- Ocelot: kitten
- Opossum: joey
- Otter: pup, whelp
- Owl: owlet, fledgling
- Oyster: spat
- Penguin: chick, nestling
- Pigeon: squab, squeaker
- Porcupine: pup
- Rabbit: bunny, kit, kitten
- Raccoon: cub, kit
- Rhinoceros: calf
- Seahorse: seafoal
- Shark: cub, pup
- Skunk: kit
- Sloth: baby, kitten, pup
- Spider: spiderling
- Squirrel: kit, kitten, pup
- Tasmanian devil: joey
- Toad: tadpole, toadlet
- Wallaby: joey
- Whale: calf
- Wombat: joey
- Zebra: colt (male), filly (female), foal

Animal groups

Again, this isn't an all-encompassing list, but it's always nice to know exactly what to call a gathering of the animals you're writing about. Not to mention the fun you'll have at cocktail parties casually mentioning your clowder of cats at home, the army of frogs in your garden, or the murder of crows in your neighborhood.

Mammals

- Antelope: a herd
- Apes: a shrewdness or troop
- Badgers: a cete or colony
- Bats: a cauldron or colony
- Bears: a sloth or sleuth
- Beavers: a colony or family
- Buffalo: a gang or obstinacy
- Camels: a caravan, train, or flock
- Cats: a clowder, pounce, or glaring; for kittens: a kindle, litter, or intrigue
- Cheetahs: a coalition
- Chickens: a brood or peep
- Chicks: a clutch or chattering
- Coyotes: a band
- Deer: a herd
- Dogs: a litter (puppies) or pack (wild)
- Dolphins: a pod

- Donkeys: a pace or herd
- Elephants: a parade, herd, or memory
- Elk: a gang or herd
- Ferrets: a business
- Fox: a leash, skulk, or earth
- Giraffes: a tower
- Goats: a tribe, trip, herd, or flock
- Gorillas: a band or troop
- Hippopotamuses: a bloat or thunder
- Hyenas: a cackle or clan
- Jaguars: a shadow
- Kangaroos: a troop, mob, or herd
- Lemurs: a conspiracy
- Leopards: a leap
- Lions: a pride or sawt
- Martens: a richness
- Mice: a nest, mischief, horde, or pack
- Moles: a labor
- Monkeys: a troop or barrel
- Mules: a pack, span, or barren
- Otters: a romp, bevy, family, or raft
- Pigs: a drift, drove, sounder, team, or passel
- Porcupines: a prickle
- Porpoises: a pod, school, herd, or turmoil
- Prairie dogs: a coterie

- Rabbits: a colony, warren, nest, down, husk, or herd (domestic only)
- Raccoons: a gaze
- Rats: a colony, pack, plague, or swarm
- Rhinoceroses: a crash
- Seals: a pod
- Sharks: a shiver
- Sheep: a drove, flock, hurtle, fold, or pack
- Skunks: a surfeit
- Squirrels: a dray or scurry
- Tigers: an ambush or streak
- Walruses: a herd or pod
- Weasels: a gang, pack, confusion, sneak, or boogle
- Whales: a pod, gam, herd, school, or mod
- Wombats: a wisdom, mob, or colony
- Wolves: a pack, rout, or route (when in movement)
- Zebras: a herd

Birds

- Albatross: a rookery
- Bitterns: a sedge
- Buzzards: a wake
- Bobolinks: a chain
- Coots: a cover
- Cormorants: a gulp

- Crows: a murder or horde
- Dotterel: a trip
- Doves: a dule or pitying (specific to turtle doves)
- Ducks: a brace, team, flock (in flight), raft, or paddling (on water)
- Eagles: a convocation
- Emus: a mob
- Falcons: a cast
- Finches: a charm
- Flamingos: a stand
- Geese: a flock, gaggle (on the ground), or skein (in flight)
- Grouse: a pack (in late season)
- Gulls: a colony or screech
- Hawks: a cast, kettle (in flight), or boil (two or more spiraling in air)
- Herons: a sedge or siege
- Hummingbirds: a charm
- Jays: a party or scold
- Lapwings: a deceit
- Larks: an exaltation
- Mallards: a sord (in flight) or brace
- Magpies: a tiding, gulp, murder, or charm
- Nightingales: a watch
- Owls: a parliament
- Parrots: a pandemonium or company
- Partridge: a covey

- Peacocks: an ostentation or muster
- Penguins: a colony, muster, parcel, or rookery
- Pheasant: a nest, nide (a brood), nye, or bouquet
- Plovers: a congregation or wing (in flight)
- Ptarmigans: a covey
- Quail: a bevy or covey
- Ravens: an unkindness
- Rooks: a building
- Snipe: a walk or wisp
- Sparrows: a host
- Starlings: a murmuration or chattering
- Storks: a mustering
- Swans: a bevy, game, or wedge (in flight)
- Teal: a spring
- Turkeys: a rafter, gang, or posse
- Woodcocks: a fall
- Woodpeckers: a descent

Reptiles and amphibians

- Alligators: a congregation
- Cobras: a quiver
- Crocodiles: a bask or float
- Frogs: an army, colony, or knot
- Lizards: a lounge
- Rattlesnakes: a rhumba

- Salamanders: a maelstrom or congress
- Snakes: a nest, den, pit, bed, or knot
- Toads: a knot
- Turtles: a bale or nest

Fishes

- Fishes in general: a draft, nest, run, school, or shoal
- Herring: an army
- Salmon: a run
- Sharks: a shiver, school, or shoal
- Stingrays: a fever
- Trout: a hover

Invertebrates

- Ants: a colony, army, swarm, or nest
- Bees: a grist, hive, swarm, or nest
- Butterflies: a flight or flutter
- Caterpillars: an army
- Clams: a bed
- Cockroaches: an intrusion
- Crabs: a cast or consortium
- Flies: a business, swarm, or cloud
- Gnats: a cloud, horde, or swarm
- Grasshoppers: a cloud
- Hornets: a nest or bike

- Jellyfish: a bloom, fluther, or smack

- Lobsters: a risk

- Oysters: a bed

- Scorpions: a bed or nest

- Snails: a hood

- Spiders: a cluster or clutter

- Squid: an audience

- Termites: a colony, nest, swarm, or brood

- Wasps: a nest or swarm

- Worms: a bed, clew, bunch, or clat

Exceptions to the rule: your characters

While these words may be the correct way to refer to groups of various animal species, we might imagine a scenario in which these words are intentionally avoided. For example, let's suppose a character is trying to convince others that a group of whales is in many ways like a group of humans. Perhaps you'd repeat "group" to emphasize similarities instead of differences.

Also, a scientist or word geek might be someone who always uses these terms correctly, while a layperson may not.

A few resources

If you're writing about an animal species that isn't as well known as our domestic companions or familiar wildlife, you'll need to do some research.

> A writer needs three things: experience, observation, and imagination, any two of which, at times, can supply the lack of the others. —William Faulkner

As a writer seeking information about animals, you have three main avenues to acquire such information—reference research (books, the internet, film, videos, and other media), in-person research (which entails interviews with other humans), and field research (which means traveling, observing animals in their natural habitats, and observing and exploring this habitat).

We'll dive more into research next, in Part 3, where you'll find tips for doing all these types of research. In the meantime, below are a few book resources for you to check out as you explore animal lives. This list is by no means comprehensive, but these books—by journalists, scientists, and animal advocates— offer insights into myriad species. Visit EcoLitBooks.com for additional titles, plus new and ongoing book reviews in every genre of environmental and animal literature.

Animal studies & observations

Bitch: On the Female of the Species by Lucy Cooke

Wildlife Spectacles: Mass Migrations, Mating Rituals, and Other Fascinating Animal Behaviors by Vladimir Dinets

How Animals Grieve by Barbara J. King

Trash Animals: How We Live with Nature's Filthy, Feral, Invasive, and Unwanted Species edited by Kelsi Nagy and Phillip David Johnson II

Becoming Wild: How Animal Cultures Raise Families, Create Beauty, and Achieve Peace by Carl Safina

Sea animals

What a Fish Knows: The Inner Lives of Our Underwater Cousins by Jonathan Balcombe

Other Minds: The Octopus, the Sea, and the Deep Origins of Consciousness by Peter Godfrey-Smith

Return of the Sea Otter: The Story of the Animal That Evaded Extinction on the Pacific Coast by Todd McLeish

The Soul of an Octopus: A Surprising Exploration into the Wonders of Consciousness by Sy Montgomery

Birds

The Meaning of Birds by Simon Barnes

Where Song Began: Australia's Birds and How They Changed the World by Tim Low

Land animals

American Wolf: A True Story of Survival and Obsession in the West by Nate Blakeslee

Koala: A Natural History and an Uncertain Future by Danielle Clode

Ice Bear: The Cultural History of an Arctic Icon by Michael Engelhard

Coyote America: A Natural and Supernatural History by Dan Flores

Eager: The Surprising, Secret Life of Beavers and Why They Matter by Ben Goldfarb

Insects

The Insect Crisis: The Fall of the Tiny Empires that Run the World by Oliver Milman

Part 3:
The Craft of Animal Writing

Introduction

At this point in your journey you probably have an idea of what you want to write (fiction, nonfiction, poetry) and who or what you want to write about. You might even have a desired outcome for your writing.

Now it's time to put pencil or pen to paper—or fingers to keyboards—and start exploring the craft of animal writing.

The craft of writing, like the craft of cooking or woodworking, requires an understanding of all the tools and techniques at your disposal. The good news here is that you don't need to purchase a table saw or a new oven to get started.

But you do need to be patient and persistent. The best chefs and cabinetmakers did not become the best in a week or two—or a month. They got there by practice, by working every day, by learning from their mistakes, and by studying the work of others.

Think about the types of literature, art, and film that inspire you to create. Think about your favorite novels, movies, and TV shows. Why do they stand apart to you? Is it place? Is it the story itself? Is it the characters?

Whether you are writing fiction or nonfiction, you will need to consider all the elements of story, including character, plot, dialogue, setting and detail, and your audience. And in order to tell your stories, you'll likely need to do plenty of research. This section covers it all, with a focus on writing for animals.

Story

"The cat sat on the mat is not a story. The cat sat on the other cat's mat is a story." —John le Carré

Anyone who has known or lived with felines will appreciate this quote from John le Carré—and will recognize it for the great drama that it evokes. And it's meant to remind us that writing for animals—like all writing—is about story.

But we also should remember that stories are everywhere. Even the seemingly mundane act of telling someone about your day is a sort of storytelling: what happened at work, at school, with the kids, with the companion animals. So keep in mind that while your first order of business as a writer is to create and tell a story, it's not as onerous as it may seem.

Stories are what readers connect to, and stories exist in all genres, whether you're writing a novel or an op-ed or a poem. In fiction, you'll be creating characters from which your plot will emerge. If you're writing nonfiction, you're not simply relaying events but developing them in a way that reveals a beginning, middle, and end.

While both fiction and nonfiction will feature characters, action, and consequences, there are myriad options. In fiction, for example, you can make use of different genres to tell animals' stories: romance, adventure, literary, mystery. In Armand Chauvel's novel *The Green and the Red*, a vegetarian and carnivore fall in love—and in Gwyn Hyman Rubio's

Love and Ordinary Creatures, a cockatoo is in love with his human caretaker (and very jealous of her human love interest). Deb Olin Unferth's novel *Barn 8* is about animal activists undertaking a daring chicken rescue, and Katy Yocom's novel *Three Ways to Disappear* seamlessly weaves together the stories of sisters, family tragedy, and tiger conservation. There are no limits to the ways in which animal protection can be woven into—or be a central part of—any fictional story.

In nonfiction, you may be writing a personal story about an encounter that changed your view about how animals are treated, or an op-ed with a clear call to action, such as how to help save the wolves. And if you're writing a news or feature article, keep in mind that individual stories are so much more accessible and meaningful to readers than data (which is also important in its own right). As one example, in *Phoenix Zones: Where Strength Is Born and Resilience Lives*, author Hope Ferdowsian offers the statistic that more than sixty billion animals are killed each year for food, about ten billion in the U.S. alone, and then goes on to tell the story of Julia, a pig in a factory farm who was brutally abused before she was rescued by Farm Sanctuary. Ferdowsian describes Julia and what she endured, noting that by having a chance to recover and heal, she is one of the very few lucky ones out of these billions of animals. These staggering numbers are made real by learning of this individual pig's harrowing journey from farm to sanctuary, and it makes readers think of the billions of others who are not so fortunate.

Story, of course, doesn't exist on its own—in fact, all stories begin with character (see the next chapter). In the coming chapters we'll also get into other elements of story, including plot, dialogue, setting and detail, and considering your audience.

- Tell a story about one or more animals—for example, something that happened among your companion animals, witnessing an encounter among animals in the wild, or an observation of insects in your home or yard. Write a scene describing what you think is going on among the animals.

- Next, consider genre. In what genre do you think this story might fit best?

- Finally, have some fun with genre. If your story is a literary one, make it a romance. If it's a romance, make it a mystery or a thriller—and so on.

✎ WRITING PROMPT

- Find and reflect on a statistic about animals—for example, that 46 million turkeys are slaughtered in the U.S. for Thanksgiving each year, or that 150 species go extinct globally every day.

- Create a character based on one of these animals.

- Write a scene featuring this character.

Character (human and nonhuman)

Stories are what readers connect to—and even more, readers connect to characters, who are the foundation of all stories. This section will be devoted to tips and tools for creating strong human and nonhuman characters when writing for animals.

As a literary activist, your goal is to create—or, in the case of nonfiction, portray—characters who pull readers in and open their minds and hearts to animal issues. And because characters are at the heart of all good stories, characterization is an essential first step, no matter what your book or story will be about.

If you're writing nonfiction, you'll want to identify, study, and reveal the issues through the players involved. For example, if you profile a sanctuary for a magazine, focus on the human and nonhuman animals who inhabit this place. If you're writing about anything from farming to rescue, taking a close look at the animals (again, both human and nonhuman) will be what captures readers, even more than the facts or data (though these can be useful and important as well).

Below are a few tips for how to create or portray characters without being preachy or didactic in your writing. The best animal writing will enlighten by drawing readers into the story, not by overtly advocating a certain message.

Have a diverse set of characters

In both fiction and nonfiction, you'll want characters along a wide spectrum so that your readers will have someone with whom to identify. Better yet, having characters with diverse lives and opinions leads to conflict, which is essential in any story.

Consider Barbara Kingsolver's environmental novel *Flight Behavior*, in which the main character, Dellarobia, becomes interested in science and climate change in a setting in which she is the only local who is concerned about it. For most of the people in her town, "weather is the Lord's business," and they don't want to consider not logging because their lives depend on it. Due to her new interests, Dellarobia becomes a bit of an outsider in her own hometown—yet at the same time, she's also an outsider among the environmental activists, who circulate a pledge to lower one's carbon footprint by doing such things as bringing Tupperware to restaurants for leftovers, eating less red meat, and shopping at secondhand stores. To Dellarobia, all of these things are completely irrelevant to her and many others in town—she hasn't eaten in a restaurant in years, doesn't eat meat because it's too expensive, and always shops secondhand because that's all she can afford. The juxtaposition between the locals and the visiting environmentalists and researchers creates drama and tension as well as provides a close look at the issues and the stakes involved—all seamlessly revealed through the characters and their stories.

In J.M. Coetzee's novel *Elizabeth Costello*, Elizabeth Costello's son is caught between his mother and his wife, as his mother advocates for animals and her daughter-in-law goes into "a fury and will not give it up." This power struggle reveals both sides of animal rights issues through family drama that readers are likely to relate to; through these well-drawn characters, Coetzee is able to highlight animal rights concerns without ever sacrificing story.

✎ WRITING PROMPT

- Write about a vegan and an omnivore having a meal together. What is said between them? What is unsaid?

- Next, rewrite the scene from another point of view—if it was from the vegan's point of view, write from the omnivore's, or vice versa. How does this change the mood of the scene?

Characters, human and nonhuman, should have an arc

Your main character should grow, learn, and change during the course of the story: A character who begins the story at Point A should end up at Point B, or Point R, or Point Z. Your character's journey can be physical, mental, emotional, cultural, and/or all of the above.

To return to *Flight Behavior*, for example, the novel opens with Dellarobia heading into the mountains to have an affair to escape her stifling life; her character arc begins when she sees a huge swarm of monarch butterflies, which brings scientists to her small Appalachian town—and from this point on she begins to change as what happens in the novel unfolds and causes her to reexamine everything in her life.

Character arcs are not only for human characters—as Hannah Sandoval points out in her essay on *Cujo* ("Rabies Bites: How Stephen King Made a Dog a Compelling Main Character") in *Writing for Animals*, the dog in this novel succeeds as a character in part because he has an arc (though as Sandoval notes, in Cujo's case, it's sadly more of a downward spiral). Depending on the animals featured in your work and how major their characters are to the narrative, you should consider their arcs throughout the course of the story.

✏ WRITING PROMPT

- Write about your favorite animal when you were five years old, then twelve, then eighteen. (Feel free to add additional ages, about five to seven years apart, depending on how old you are now.)

- Write about your favorite animal now.

- How has your relationship with animals—or view of animals—changed over the years?

✏ WRITING PROMPT

- Write about your eating habits at the age of five, then twelve, then eighteen. (Feel free to add additional ages, about five to seven years apart, depending on how old you are now.) What were your favorite foods at each age, and why?

- Write about the way you eat now. What are your favorite foods, and why?

- How have things changed over the years—and why?

Use characters' relationships to get points across

If you have a diverse set of characters in your work, creating conflict via their relationships will come rather easily—having diverse characters with strong opinions will inevitably lead to conflict. If you're writing fiction, arrange these relationships to get ideas across (through dialogue, for example). If you're writing nonfiction, highlight relationships that might in turn highlight the issues.

By putting characters in challenging relationships, you can tackle issues in your writing without "telling" readers about the issues and, most important, without coming across as preachy. Your characters, if they are vivid and authentic, will do all this work for you.

As Beth Lyons explains in her essay "Real Advocacy within Fantasy Worlds" in *Writing for Animals*, she uses characters' differences to create conflict: "My healer, Indira, would explain her world view to another character (and therefore to the reader). If one character is a vegan healer, the other one could be a meat-eating thief. Opposites attract, and more important, opposites allow for exposition."

So, you might put a vegan into a relationship with a non-vegan; you might create a sympathetic farmer. Try putting characters on opposite sides of an issue—or, just as effective, create conflict between characters who are on the same side. In Ann Pancake's novel *Strange as This Weather Has*

Been, the characters who inhabit the West Virginia town in which the book is set see their environment being destroyed by mountaintop removal mining—and yet, like those in Kingsolver's *Flight Behavior*, many of them aren't ready to fight for the land, as precious as it is; they are desperate for the work that mining jobs provide.

Similarly, in Karen Joy Fowler's *We Are All Completely Beside Ourselves*, in a family that has lost a nonhuman family member, the characters have different ways of coping with their loss. The narrator, Rosemary, grew up not seeing the difference between human and nonhuman animals and mourns the loss of her sister. Her father, a scientist, "was kind to animals unless it was in the interest of science to be otherwise." Her brother, stunned by the treatment of his nonhuman sister, becomes an ALF activist. Throughout the novel, the discussions, arguments, and actions of these characters serve to expose how we as a society treat animals.

✏ WRITING PROMPT

- Think of a job you imagine you would hate doing, whether for ethical or personal reasons, because you feel you may not be good at it, or whatever the case may be.

- Then, write about a day in your life doing this job.

- Finally, write a scene in which you tell someone who knows you well about your day.

Play against type

If you're writing a work of activist literature for mainstream readers, it's especially important to show that not every environmentalist wears hemp and eats nothing but tofu and wheatgrass (yes, there are still folks who actually believe this!). Similarly, not every oil-industry executive has to wear wool suits and watch Fox News—and not every passionate activist is a twentysomething, as mainstream fiction tends to portray them. By avoiding—or flipping—certain stereotypes, you're not only creating complex and interesting characters but you're challenging readers to pay closer attention to them because they are not, at a glance, what they may seem.

In Coetzee's novel *Elizabeth Costello*, the main character is an activist in her sixties who believes "I'm too old not to say these things." Likewise, in Olga Tokarczuk's novel *Drive Your Plow Over the Bones of the Dead*, the narrator Janina is an older woman standing up for animals in a village of hunters.

✎ WRITING PROMPT

- Write about a Wall Street hedge fund manager who is a passionate vegan.
- Write about a spiritual healer who is miserly.
- Write about a trust-fund college student who is humble and generous.
- Write about a dedicated volunteer with the elderly who is estranged from her parents.
- Write about a billionaire who lives very modestly.

Creating vegan characters

One question that will come up for writer-activists is whether their characters should be vegan and how to portray this in the story without turning off those who find the very word *vegan* to be preachy. The best answer to this question is to be true to your characters and what they stand for. Naturally, an animal rights activist will be vegan—but how far should you go in describing what they eat? And what about other characters who may be at different places along the animal rights spectrum, or nowhere near it?

Two-thirds of the way through the writing of her first novel, Beth Lyons realized something, which she describes in her essay "Real Advocacy within Fantasy Worlds" in *Writing for Animals*: "One of my main characters, a magical healer named Indira, hadn't eaten anything. Ever. Almost 70,000 words, and the poor woman hadn't even nibbled on a crust of bread."

As a vegan, Lyons had avoided food in her narrative, unsure how to approach it in a fantasy novel in which characters would normally hunt and kill their food. And it brought her to the question: "Do vegan writers have a duty to present vegan options in their stories, or can they simply tell their stories and leave real-world politics alone?"

Lyons chose to take the opportunity to expand her fictional world, as well as perhaps her readers' mindsets, and this is an opportunity we can all try to take—if we can do it effectively and authentically. That is, any references to veganism in fiction should be true to the characters and the story so that it's a natural part of the narrative and not a preachy aside.

As Lyons mentions in her essay, it's tempting to avoid the topic altogether—but if we're creating enough detail in our work, food *will* come up, whether it's a character cooking at home, a group of friends out on the town, or a couple having a romantic dinner. So when you put characters at a table together, you should consider the setting and context, what's important in the scene, and how much detail you need to go into to make it both relevant and authentic.

Though we've all likely encountered preachy vegans in real life, we recommend avoiding this in fiction, as it's a stereotype that the animals and the planet really could do without. On the other hand, portraying vegans as saints doesn't reflect reality either. No matter how you describe food and a character's diet in your work, be sure that it's a reflection of the character and not a public service announcement.

You can show both sides of the issue, as John did in his novel *The Tourist Trail*, in which one of the main characters becomes vegan by necessity—his undercover job depends on it. The novel shows the character's ignorance, adjustment period, and then his embracing of veganism (which was aided by a vegan love interest—this always helps!). This character's journey echoes that of many humans on their way to veganism— it happens in stages, with a bit of skepticism and plenty of mistakes along the way.

In Midge's novel *My Last Continent*, the penguin researcher Deb is a vegan in a meat-eating world, and for the most part Midge chose the subtle route when it comes to what Deb eats, with descriptions of vegan food (from toast and fruit for breakfast to pasta for dinner) without making a point about it being vegan, except in a couple of key moments. This subtle approach works well if you want to be true to your character's sensibility but not call it out in a big way, which may be jarring for readers if it's not a crucial element of a scene.

✐ WRITING PROMPT

- Write a time you changed someone's mind about something, or they changed yours. Feel free to write this as a fictional scene if you've got a work in progress—or write it as a fantasy if you've been trying to change someone's mind but haven't been able to.

- Note: What was the catalyst for change?

- Also: How long did it take? (One conversation, a decade, etc.)

✐ WRITING PROMPT

- Take a scene in your work in progress that needs more detail about food, whether a picnic, a day at work, a first date, or a holiday. Describe what each character is eating.

- Next, consider the extent to which what your characters eat reveals who they are. For example, does someone who prefers a vegan diet eat meat or dairy to please someone else? Does food cause conflict in any of these situations? To what extent do the characters think about what they eat, i.e., is food a moral issue, mere sustenance, etc.?

Nonhuman animals as characters

It's challenging enough for us writers to create authentic human characters in our work—even more challenging is giving voices to nonhuman animals while honoring who they are. This is because it's impossible, as a different species, to truly know them the way we can know our fellow humans.

For one, animals do not speak our language—so this makes translation especially challenging. As Hannah Sandoval points out in her *Writing for Animals* essay about *Cujo*: "Animals do not think in words because they do not speak. Giving your animal character actual thought quotes is unrealistic."

Sandoval also adds that putting animals' thoughts into simplistic language will render them childish or cartoonish rather than compelling characters in their own right—this does far more of a disservice to animals than not writing about them at all.

Sandoval notes that the actions and behaviors of animals are far more familiar to readers than things we cannot see—and this is a great place to begin writing your animal character. By using actions as well as language, perhaps even more than language, nonhuman characters will be familiar to human readers in a way that we can understand. We as humans cannot know how animals' voices might sound, but we will recognize how they act.

In his short story "Litter" (in *Among Animals*), Philip Armstrong uses action as well as the second-person voice to put readers directly into the mind and body of a stray dog. When Armstrong writes, "You uncurl your rib-marked body, get to your feet and slowly stretch, back legs, front legs," anyone who's ever observed a dog standing and stretching after a nap will recognize this action. Further into the story, Armstrong goes deeper into the dog's emotional world—but by beginning with small dog actions, he eases readers into the animal's point of view seamlessly and authentically. We readers can relate to the physical details so well that it's easier and more credible when we transition into how the dog thinks and feels. The actions help get us into the mindset of a dog, and the second-person point of view helps put readers directly into this animal's paws.

And of course, don't be afraid to expand your reach, if the animal and credibility allow—and if you do, do this early and with authority. In her novel *Love and Ordinary Creatures*, bestselling author Gwyn Hyman Rubio boldly created a nonhuman character who carries the entire novel. In this opening scene, Rubio introduces us to the book's narrator, Caruso, who is a sulfur-crested cockatoo.

> If [Caruso] dared, he would undo the snap hook and lock, steal through the cage door, and nest in [Clarissa's] hair. If he dared, he would escape, not to the open sky but to her open palms ... but then if he dared, she would know that he is smarter than all the authorities of books on psittacids suggest he is—that he is smarter than the porpoise, the whale, the gorilla, and Ruthie, the four-year-old girl who lives next door. "Claaa-risss-a," he says a little louder.

Readers see straightaway that Caruso is not only establishing himself as the narrator of the book, but he's also letting us know that we're in capable hands. Rubio uses science to show how smart he is, and Caruso's love for Clarissa, his human caretaker, shows that he is capable of emotion.

If you have an animal as a main character, as Hannah Sandoval has noted, he/she/they should have a character arc like any human character. In *Love and Ordinary Creatures*, for example, we see Caruso evolve from a charming yet single-minded and cunning individual to an amazingly humble and generous one by the end of the novel.

And finally, remember that part of our jobs as writers is to read—a lot. And as you focus on writing for animals, always keep an eye out for how other writers portray animals— what they do well and also what they get wrong. This sort of writerly reading helps us become better at what we do.

It's especially interesting to note the compassionate treatment of animals in books that aren't focused on animals or animal protection—for example, Sigrid Nunez's novel *What Are You Going Through* contains a scene told from the point of view of a cat who'd had a rough previous life on the streets. The book's title and theme come from an epigraph by Simone Weil: "The love of our neighbor in all its fullness simply means being able to say to him, 'What are you going through?'"—and it's beautiful to see that Nunez has extended this to animals in this particular scene.

Even big-game hunter Ernest Hemingway, in his story "The Short Happy Life of Francis Macomber," includes a surprisingly empathetic moment told from the point of view of a lion who has just been shot on safari.

In many cases, scenes in non-animal-focused work are more in service of the human narrators—but they are nonetheless significant in that they connect humans to nonhumans, and for many mainstream readers this is an important connection to make. And it's always worth paying attention to how writers handle animals in their work—whether it shows us what's possible or whether it inspires us to do better.

It's also good to remember that even when you're writing something that isn't specifically animal-centric, you still may have opportunities in your non-animal writing to enlighten readers to animal issues. In fact, sometimes a more subtle approach works very well.

✎ WRITING PROMPT

- Write a scene from the point of view of a nonhuman animal, whether it's your companion animal or a wild animal, a snail in your garden or a cow at a farm.

  Part 1: Begin with a detailed description of this animal's world.

  Part 2: Bring another being into this animal's word—perhaps it's another animal of the same species, or one of a different species, or a human. What happens when this encounter occurs?

  Part 3: Take a few brief notes on this prompt and what it revealed to you.

- Observe a species of animal—from cows to pigs to chickens—on a factory farm and describe what you see, everything from living conditions to animal behavior. (If you're not able to do this firsthand, watch footage of farmed animals, which you can find on any number of websites, such as Mercy for Animals, PETA, and Free from Harm.)

- Next, visit an animal sanctuary and observe the same species in this environment. (If you're unable to visit a local sanctuary in person, watch videos online or via social media by virtually visiting a rescue such as Farm Sanctuary, Woodstock Farm Sanctuary, or NSW Hen Rescue.)

✐ WRITING PROMPT

- Think of (or go read) a book written from an animal's point of view. Take a few moments to write about how this book resonated with you. What does the author get right? Where does the characterization fall short?

Plot

Plot includes the events that make up your story—the many things that happen along the way.

While many writers begin a story by developing plot, the best way to begin is with character. If you've got a set of strong, diverse, interesting characters, your plot will reveal itself.

> I say don't worry about plot. Worry about the characters. Let what they say or do reveal who they are, and be involved in their lives, and keep asking yourself, Now what happens? ... Find out what each character cares about most in the world because then you will have discovered what's at stake. —Anne Lamott, *Bird by Bird*

Whether human or nonhuman, every individual has a life that's important, and when things get in the way (of their freedom, of what they want or need), this is how plot is born. Focus on your characters and what happens to them, and your plot will evolve from there.

In Philip Armstrong's short story, "Litter," the dog character wants safety, food, shelter—only to find herself in a home that is in many ways worse than being on the street.

In Gwyn Hyman Rubio's *Love and Ordinary Creatures*, Caruso the cockatoo wants to be loved, and many things get in the way of the love he wants from his human caretaker, offering both humor and pathos as the story heads toward its dramatic conclusion.

In Olga Tokarczuk's novel *Drive Your Plow Over the Bones of the Dead*, the human narrator, Janina, wants law enforcement to do something about poaching, and when no one listens to her, this creates the novel's wonderfully dark and mysterious plot.

When talking about plot, Kurt Vonnegut said that all characters must want something, even if it's a glass of water.

✎ WRITING PROMPT

- Consider three major characters within your story. Write the following about each of them:
  - ○ What does each of them want?
  - ○ Is this the same or different from what they need?
  - ○ What is getting in their way?

✎ WRITING PROMPT

- Write about an animal you've observed recently, whether your companion animal, a neighbor's dog, a deer in the forest, or a snail in your garden.
- Imagine what you think this animal wanted or needed in the moments you observed him/her.
- Finally, write about the animal getting what he/she wanted or needed.

Dialogue

In fiction, dialogue does three important things: It helps define characters, it moves the story forward, and it provides a variety of structure and language.

In nonfiction, dialogue accomplishes all of the above with quotations from real humans rather than the made-up dialogue of fictional characters. In nonfiction, quotes would be in an interview format (in a news story or feature, for example), or may be written as real-life scenes recorded by the writer (as in long-form narrative journalism). In memoir, dialogue may comprise remembered conversations among the real-life inhabitants of the writer's life. Most important, quotations in nonfiction allow readers to hear people's voices, which lends authority if it's an expert, portrays emotion if it's a story, and so on.

In fiction, dialogue is quite simple: It's what your characters say. So, whether you're writing fiction or nonfiction, you'll want to be sure that readers can hear the players in the story talking.

When it comes to defining character, dialogue helps portray personality and backstory through such things as speech patterns, language, and dialect. When we hear characters speak, we learn things such as where they're from (based on accents and dialect), their education level (based on word choices and syntax), their attitude and worldview (through voice and tone—i.e., what they say and how they say it), and a character's mood in the moment (the differences between how they speak at any given time to any given person).

Another wonderful thing about dialogue is that it allows a viewpoint that's different from being inside characters' heads—for example, it allows us to see what characters think versus what they say. We can see when characters are hiding something; we can see them lie. Such literary devices help build tension and create conflict in a story.

Dialogue is also a very effective way to move your story forward. Through dialogue, readers see the story unfolding in "real time" because conversation can be more lively and interactive than interior monologue (i.e., simply "telling" a reader what a character is thinking).

As mentioned above, dialogue provides an excellent way to show conflict, and nothing propels a story forward like conflict. Dialogue is effective for portraying arguments, of course, but also consider how one character's silence may be just as effective in revealing tension.

When written well and true to character, dialogue also helps get across the themes of your work; often, revealing animal issues risks sounding preachy when woven into the narrative, but if a certain issue is tackled in dialogue—such as through an argument between two characters—it ends up coming across as so much more real.

Finally, dialogue provides a variety of structure and language—which may not seem important but is definitely something to consider, as readers appreciate prose that keeps them engaged. According to Stephen King, who has no trouble keeping readers engaged: "Paragraphs are almost always as important for how they look as for what they say."

So if you find yourself with characters who are thinking more than talking, or when you have long passages of prose that slow down the narrative, see how dialogue might liven up your story and move things along—and this will also provide a reader-friendly visual element that helps keep readers immersed in the story.

With all these things in mind, note that dialogue first and foremost must serve the characters and the story—not the author or the author's agenda. Use dialogue when it allows you to accomplish the goals above—but only when it's appropriate for the characters and the context.

✎ WRITING PROMPT

- Describe someone using only dialogue (for example, write a conversation in which two characters gossip about another, or write about a character telling a story about themselves). If you've got a work in progress, you can apply this prompt to a fictional character, or the subject of an interview or essay.

✎ WRITING PROMPT

- Write a conversation you'd like to have with your companion animal(s).

- What would you most want them to hear?

- What would you most want to understand about them?

Setting & detail

When it comes to writing for animals, setting and detail are especially important, particularly when you're writing for mainstream audiences who may not be aware of animal issues. You'll need to clearly articulate why these issues are important without being didactic, and using details can show readers these issues firsthand.

In one exceptional moment in her novel *Drive Your Plow Over the Bones of the Dead*, Olga Tokarczuk's narrator Janina tries to get people to see how they've become immune to compassion by exhorting them to really think about what they eat. It is murder, she insists; it is a crime, yet no one acknowledges it. Janina asks: "When you walk past a shop window where large chunks of butchered bodies are hanging on display, do you stop to wonder what it really is?"

Another effective way to use detail is to show not only the abuses of animals but their extraordinary lives and personalities—that is, show readers who they are and reveal that they are not so unlike human animals. In *Barn 8*, Deb Olin Unferth not only reveals the brutality of factory farming but she also works in fascinating details about chickens. When she writes, "Chickens gossip, summon, play, flirt, teach, warn, mourn, fight, praise, and promise," readers can see them as sentient beings and empathize with these smart and emotional animals being deprived of the most basic of freedoms.

Setting as well as detail helps to show animals' personalities, traits, and culture. Learn as much as you can about an animal's natural habitat, and always gather more information than you think you'll need. You never know what you might include: natural history, weather, the humans and nonhumans among them. The more information you have, the better you'll be able to portray the animals in your work.

Of course, always keep the details and settings you portray relevant to the characters (human or nonhuman) and the story. If you have more research than you need, you may be tempted to throw it all in there—resist that temptation! When researching *My Last Continent*, Midge ended up learning far more about penguins than she could ever use, so she had to choose carefully so as to include only what was most relevant to the story. As one example, she realized that the mating habits of one species of Antarctic penguin closely resembled the relationship of two human characters in the story. The Adélie penguins, she learned, will sometimes mate for life, but they are loyal first and foremost to their nesting sites; when Adélies return to their nests, if their partners don't show, they choose new ones and move on. As it turned out, the love story between two of the humans in the novel was not unlike the Adélie penguins; early in the novel, Deb and Keller are both more loyal to their work on the continent than to each other, which creates much of the conflict in the early stages of their relationship. Making this connection to the birds not only provided a parallel but also shows that humans and nonhumans are truly not as different as we may think.

A very important part of setting and detail is to use all five senses. Every reader experiences what they read differently, so include all that you can, which will not only add dimension to your writing but will appeal to a wider variety of readers.

Keep in mind that you don't want to describe a place using all five senses in one giant paragraph; whether you're writing a short story or a novel, sprinkle your description throughout.

Use sight, sound, smell, taste, and touch—but don't neglect to consider the sixth sense as well, the intangibles that we feel but don't experience with the other five senses.

One final note about details: As mentioned in Part 2, take good care with how you use words and idioms. Don't perpetuate animal stereotypes or adages, and choose your words carefully. In *Writing for Animals*, Beth Lyons writes about replacing the word *waterskin* for *canteen* in her fantasy novel, to be more animal-friendly. These seemingly small word choices are actually quite important, and the more we can get away from using them, the more empathy all humans will have toward nonhuman animals.

✐ WRITING PROMPT

- Write about a time you learned something new about animals: where it was, how you learned it, what the context was (being taught, personal observation, etc.).

- Next, write about the sensual elements you remember, one at a time. First, the sights. Then the sounds. Then smells. Then texture. Then taste. Finally: was there a sixth sense for you?

- What was most interesting to you about this learning experience and why?

- What did it teach you—and how did it teach you? You'll want to use such details to meaningfully portray the lives of animals to your readers.

✐ WRITING PROMPT

- Write about a recent animal encounter you had—for example, with your companion animal or a pigeon in the park.

- What was the most vivid sensory element you remember, and why?

- Insert into this scene a different sensory element, even if you have to imagine the details.

✐ WRITING PROMPT

- Find a scene in your work in progress that needs more detail.

- Next, spend five minutes each on the sensory details of where the scene is set.

- First, write about the sights of the place—again, for no fewer than five minutes. Then write about the sounds. Then the smells. Then the textures of the place. Then the tastes associated with the place. Finally, write about the sixth sense, the emotional feel of the place (consider cultural history, the backstory of the characters, etc.).

- Finally, edit the scene so only the most vivid and relevant senses remain in the scene. (And recycle anything that doesn't fit so you can use it in another scene!)

✐ WRITING PROMPT

- Write a scene featuring an animal, or take a scene from your work in progress, and rewrite this scene so that it takes place: in rain, in daylight, at midnight, in a snow squall, at sunset, and so on.

✐ WRITING PROMPT

- Think of an animal you know well. Write about your favorite details—for example, the "toe beans" of a cat or the eyelashes of a cow.

- Think of an animal you don't know well. Find photos and/or videos online and choose a detail about the animal to describe.

Audience

"Write with the door closed; rewrite with the door open." —Stephen King

When you are in the process of writing, it's best not to let anything stop you—especially the idea of readers and what they might think of your work. But once you've gotten to a certain stage of your project—like the revision stage, as Stephen King suggests—you'll want to consider whom you're writing for, and what tweaks you need to make to your material in order to best reach that audience.

If, for example, you're writing a children's book, get to know the industry; there's a big difference between children's books (usually illustrated), middle grade books, and young adult (YA) books. Keep in mind that young audiences, ironically, can often handle truths about animals better than adult readers; they don't have decades of habits behind them, like eating meat or wearing leather, that would bring up guilt about that and cause them to turn away—instead, they are quite likely to be open to learning the realities of how animals are treated and to live in a way that feels compassionate. For younger kids, you'll want to be gentle with the harsh realities of life, avoiding overly graphic and violent scenes and imagery, but do be sure to be forthright and honest because kids have an amazing ability to see through things that adults try to sugarcoat or hide.

While kids are information sponges, adult readers may react more favorably to nuanced portrayals of animal issues. Animal rights literature causes many readers to face the ways in which they have participated in the abuse of animals—usually without knowing it, understanding it, or being able to articulate it—and this can be devastating. You'll want to rely on the strength of your story to compel them to keep reading, but be sensitive to the fact that your readers may not be in the same place you are when it comes to facing up to the ways in which we all need to be better to the nonhuman animals among us.

Along these lines, another issue to consider is whether you're writing for a vegan or an omnivorous audience. Vegans, of course, will already have a benchmark for animal issues, whereas omnivores may not be aware of what happens in factory farms or on fur farms, in the cosmetics industry, in animal entertainment, and so on. If you're writing a mainstream novel that you hope both vegans and nonvegans will enjoy, find a balance between articulating the issues and assuming some level of knowledge. Curious omnivores will look up anything they don't learn on the page, and vegans will likely just be thrilled to see animal issues addressed in fiction (we certainly are!).

If you're writing an activist piece—for example, an op-ed to protest a local coyote hunt—try to approach it from the point of view of the readers you're trying to persuade. Instead of calling hunters cruel and barbaric, for example, you might point out that killing coyotes is unnecessary in protecting wildlife, offer peaceful preventative measures instead, and show how coyotes self-regulate their populations when they are left alone.

When it comes to your audience and your readers, we have a few tips for how to open minds and hearts to the animals you're writing about.

Make use of a popular genre

As we mentioned earlier, stories come in myriad genres, and you can write about animals in whichever one best suits you. Whether you write poetry or prose, fiction or nonfiction, mysteries or romances, any genre will provide opportunities to reach existing audiences and readers who are drawn toward the genre in which you write. Our mystery novel *Devils Island* came from our wish to write a murder mystery set on a remote island, while at the same time hoping to draw attention to the plight of endangered Tasmanian devils. The result, we've found, is that mystery lovers enjoy learning about an endangered species as much as they enjoy trying to find out who the murderer is.

Be subtle

Again, you don't want to estrange readers—young or adult— by barraging them with the cruelties inflicted on animals in our society. Animal use and abuse is a part of everyday life, yet few see it or want to see it, so what you write about may be upsetting to readers. Try to ease into the topic about which you're writing, and let your story and your characters do the educating for you.

Be inclusive

If your goal is to reach mainstream readers, consider including "mainstream" characters—which, in most cultures, means characters who eat animals. Perhaps you include an omnivore who evolves during the course of the novel, giving your readers a character they identify with and can follow along with. And keep in mind that we are all at varying points of various journeys—as your characters should be as well.

Be compassionate

Most of us were not born and raised as vegans who've never impacted the life of an animal. Even the most dedicated of vegans cannot be perfect. So remember that everyone is on an individual journey and know that everyone has a different path. Be compassionate in your writing—toward animals, certainly, but toward humans and your readers as well. The best way to help create change for animals in literature is to reveal their stories in ways that help readers feel that they can be part of changing their world for the better.

✐ WRITING PROMPT

- Write about an animal you're an advocate for—whether shelter pets, wild animals in your region, or endangered species—and why.

- Next, write an op-ed style piece about why and how these animals need our help. Write one version for each of these three audiences: 1) animal activists, 2) mainstream readers, 3) children.

Research

"The truth is that there are simply going to be times when you can't go forward in your work until you find out something about the place where you grew up, when it was a railroad town, or what the early stages of shingles are like, or what your character would actually experience the first week of beauty school. So figure out who has this information and give that person a call. It's best if you can think of someone who's witty and articulate, so you can steal all of his or her material." —Anne Lamott, *Bird by Bird*

Anne Lamott is absolutely right—there are times when we can't continue writing without doing some research. You may want to begin your research even before writing, definitely during, and maybe even a bit once you've finished a draft just to be sure you've covered everything. The great thing about researching at every stage of the writing process is that you'll often learn something that takes your character and story in a direction you hadn't imagined.

The writing prompts in this section are designed not only to get you thinking about the animals you're writing about but how to get the information you need.

✍ WRITING PROMPT

- Write down three books that opened your eyes to one (or more) animals.

- Why were those books successful? How did these writers open your eyes?

Reference research

Internet, book, magazine, and film research is great—but there's no substitute for hands-on research when it comes to learning about animal behavior, so we definitely advise you to get out there into the field whenever—and wherever—you can.

And while field research is fantastic, it's also going to be necessary to supplement this with reference materials. So, go forth and surf the internet! However, do keep in mind that while internet research can be wonderful, quick, and convenient, such information can also be unreliable, slanted, or just plain incorrect. Even Wikipedia, arguably the most popular source for information on just about anything, can be misleading or factually wrong, since it's written by volunteer contributors. And Google is now using AI to answer questions you type into its search engine—and AI is far from perfect as well. Always do your due diligence when taking "factual" info from the internet.

Books by experts, academic journals, and magazine articles can be wonderful sources of facts and details. For her novel *Once There Were Wolves*, about a biologist whose team is reintroducing wolves to the Scottish Highlands, Charlotte McConaghy turned to such resources: "I read at great length about the biologists who took on the enormously difficult task of reintroducing wolves to Yellowstone. From their accounts of those trials I learned so much about the process and the animals themselves … Their stories really brought the wolves to life for me, and made me aware that each of them has their own personality, their own mysteries to fall in love with." (Read the full interview on EcoLit Books.)

Keep in mind that research doesn't have to mean nonfiction— you might also read novels and poetry, listen to music and podcasts, watch films and documentaries, and look at photos and art from the period of time or geographic area about which you're writing.

Field and in-person research

And before, after, and during your reference research, you'll do your fieldwork, which means spending time with the animals you're writing about. Unless you yourself are a naturalist, the field research you do will likely be in conjunction with in-person research—that is, in order to get access to the field, you'll connect with naturalists. Likewise, when you connect with naturalists with your questions, always ask them if you can join them in the field, if possible—there's nothing like firsthand observation to get to know a species.

Some field research may be more accessible than others. To get to know cows or chickens up close and as individuals, for example, you might volunteer at a sanctuary, where you can not only do good for the animals and the humans who rescue them but also have a chance to observe them living peacefully and exhibiting their natural behaviors.

If you need access to an unwelcoming industry for a fictional piece, you might consider pitching a nonfiction article as a way in. In order to research her novel *Barn 8*, about a daring chicken rescue, Deb Olin Unferth wrote the article "Cage Wars" for *Harper's Magazine*. As she told EcoLit Books: "The book came before the article. That is, I had the idea for the book but I needed facts ... I wanted to be as accurate as possible. Ideally, everything I described could happen. I wrote the article as a way to get [animal rights] organizations and farmers to talk to me."

✎ WRITING PROMPT

- Write a list of things you want or need to know for your current project.

- Write down the people you know (and people they know) who may be able to help you find the info you need.

If you do the prompt above, you'll soon discover that you are far better connected than you may realize. If your list of people seems short, keep thinking on it—go through your contacts list, your social media, your family tree. List not only the people you know but the people *they* know. If you stretch a bit, you'll learn that you do know people who can be in a position to help you. And most people, we've discovered, are more than willing and happy to help a writer out.

However, if you can't find anyone who can help you learn about a specific topic, don't hesitate to reach out to strangers. In all our years of writing fiction and seeking out random information, we've never been turned down by anyone when we've asked to chat with them for a book or a story. If you need to learn about animal rescue, try a sanctuary, a rescue group, or your local shelter. If you're writing a mystery and need to talk to police officers or detectives, call your local precinct and ask to do a ride-along (a public service offered by most police stations to their communities). If you need information on any given industry, call the public relations office, whether it's a hospital or a zoo or a corporation. And never forget the invaluable resources of libraries, many of which have reference librarians on staff whom you can call or email for especially hard-to-find information.

✐ WRITING PROMPT

- Write down a place, or places, you want or need to visit to inform your current project.
- Write a list of people you know who may be able to give you access to this place or these places.

When dealing with sources, whether they are family members or new friends, always thank them about a zillion times, and then thank them again. While, like any good journalist, you should never pay for information, if you're a fiction writer who wants to learn what it's like to work at a zoo, there's no harm in buying someone coffee or lunch while they talk with you. Better yet, in addition to asking for an interview, ask your source if you can shadow them on the job, which will give you insights and details you can't glean from a conversation only. See below for more on the art of shadowing.

In the rare instance that you ask for someone's time and get turned down, thank them anyway, and be sweet about it. Ask if there's someone else who might be able to help, or whether they would recommend any other resources or books.

✐ WRITING PROMPT

- Write down a list of questions you can ask the people you plan to interview.

Getting information through in-person interviews is fun, hands-on, and enlightening. (If your source is too far away to meet with in person, a face-to-face interview via Zoom or Skype is probably the best way to get the most information. And if you aren't able to shadow someone, be sure to ask such questions as: What's a typical day on the job like? What's the weirdest thing that has ever happened to you on the job? Such questions will prompt—wait for it—stories. And it's invaluable to get stories, as well as facts and details, from a source.)

And whether or not you are fortunate enough to interview people in person, here are a few tips for how to prepare and manage both the interview and your research before, during, and after you sit down for an in-person or remote interview.

Before ...

- Do as much research as you can before your meeting so that you can ask the right questions and use the time you're being given as efficiently as possible. (Always be respectful of the time people are giving you.)

- Ask if they'd recommend anything to read or research on the topic at hand before you meet—for example, websites, books, or articles.

- Put together a list of no fewer than ten questions—not to simply ask one after the other but to have handy during the interview. You'll want the interview to feel more like a conversation, but you also want to be sure you get everything you need.

- Tell your source about your project. If you're writing fiction, be clear that while you'll use anything and everything they tell you, it'll be in a completely fictional context. Along the same line, you might warn them not to tell you anything they don't want used in your work. Even though your work may be fictional, your sources need to be prepared for you to use any information they offer.

During …

- If you meet in person, try to meet on their turf, which will give you all the more information and detail because you'll be in their environment, whether work or home. If this might make your source nervous, though, choose a neutral place, at least for your first meeting.

- Make your source feel comfortable and appreciated. Anyone who takes the time to talk with you is doing you such a huge favor; show your gratitude.

- Again, the best interview is a conversation; bring all the questions for which you need answers, but stay focused on the chat at hand, listening closely and asking follow-up questions. You can check your list of questions at the end of the interview to make sure you've covered everything.

- Stay focused on what you need, but know that the things you don't even know to ask will often be the most interesting. The best answers are to the questions you haven't thought of—so, again, listen.

- If you're meeting in person, take note of all the physical details, which can be just as important as what you're being told. Use all five senses and note everything, even things that don't seem relevant at the moment. Also, ask if you can take photos and/or videos, which is a great way to have access to details later on. Take as many as you can, as appropriate, as long as your subject is comfortable. Note that these will be just for you, and don't use them for another purpose without your subject's permission.

- Bring a notebook *and* a recorder; you never know if a recorder might fail or when the sound may be bad, so write everything down also. Important: *Always ask permission to record a conversation.*

- This is so important it's worth mentioning again: listen. And affirm that you're listening: nod, smile, etc.

- Before leaving, ask: "Is there anything I forgot to ask?" This is often the best question there is. We often find that this seemingly last-minute question offers stunning information.

- Always ask if you can follow up with a phone call, email, or visit if you think of anything else, and invite them to do the same.

- If appropriate, ask if there's anyone else you might talk with as well.

After …

- Transcribe your notes as soon as possible, whether this means typing out your recording or deciphering your notebook scribbles—preferably both. The more distance between the interview and reviewing your notes, the more you'll forget. And as you do this, remember to jot down anything related to the five senses—what you observed in terms of setting and detail—and especially the sixth sense, i.e., what was the vibe?

- If there are any gaps in your information or if you have any questions, follow up as soon as possible so you won't lose touch or momentum.

- Feel free to talk to others to give you a broader view. Even professionals in the same field can have very different philosophies, worldviews, and personalities.

- Again: You can't thank people enough for sharing their time and expertise with you. After your meeting, send an email or a note—and if the research ends up in your book, when it's published,

include them in the acknowledgments and send a
complimentary copy. (Even if it's a short story or an
essay, you might want to send a copy along if you
think they'd enjoy it.)

✍ WRITING PROMPT

- Write down a list of things you'd like to know for
  your project, such as setting, detail, atmosphere, the
  humans and nonhumans who inhabit the setting of
  your story, etc.

The prompt above is meant to prepare you for fieldwork or
shadowing, which means spending a day (or more) in your
subject's life, hanging out and observing your human and/or
nonhuman sources in their natural habitat. Fieldwork allows
for much more in-depth and interesting research, in which
you'll get details you'd likely not have the opportunity to
get in an interview. Below are a few tips for preparing and
shadowing your research subjects.

- Keep in mind that if your presence will affect
  anyone other than your subject, you may need to
  get official permission (this is especially true for
  such places as hospitals, government agencies, and
  so on). Be prepared for this, follow all the rules,
  and be patient.

- Go over any guidelines beforehand, such as the
  time and length of your visit, where exactly you'll
  be, how you'll be introduced to others, whether
  you should be an observer or participant, and so

on. Note: It's usually best to simply be an observer; when people forget you're around, you get the best details. So, for example, if you're following a veterinarian around a clinic, she'll likely introduce you to her clients and ask their permission for you to be there—after that, step back and stay out of the way, and you're likely to see yourself disappear, which is when the magic reporting happens.

- Be prepared to take notes, as recording is difficult when shadowing; the sound quality is often poor, and you'll probably want to keep your distance to avoid getting in the way. If you have questions, jot them down rather than interrupt a conversation, a meeting, a surgery.

- Take photos and videos—always ask ahead of time if this will be okay—but be as unobtrusive as possible: no flash, no smartphone sounds, etc.

- Schedule time to talk after your fieldwork day—or, if you shadow someone over a period of time, try to meet at periodic intervals so you can get any questions answered along the way.

Making sense of it all

After you've done all sorts of fascinating research, the next thing to tackle will be making sense of it. If you've done your job as a researcher/reporter, you'll likely have hundreds more pages of notes than you will manuscript pages. This may sound overwhelming—but it's a good thing.

Keep in mind that just because someone gave generously of their time, you aren't obligated to use anything from your interview or fieldwork. As tempting as it is to use every single bit of information you've gleaned—and every great anecdote—your story and characters should always come first. Always keep your research details relevant to the story at hand.

On that note, it may take a few drafts before you find that your research has seamlessly woven its way into your story. All writers use a different approach to incorporating their research; you may dump it all into a file and work from there, or you may let it simmer in your mind before getting to your writing. You may refer to your notes often, or you may ignore them, unless or until you need to verify something.

Most of all, don't use research as a way to procrastinate writing (this is all too tempting, we know). Having been there ourselves (often), we have a few tips for facing the page as you research.

One, always keep your story in mind as you research; don't just do the research or fieldwork but apply what you learn a little bit every day. If you meet a spirited rescue turkey at a sanctuary, write a scene that evening describing her—everything from her physical details to her outgoing personality. If you shadow an exhausted and overworked veterinarian, weave some of this into your veterinarian character, or show the effects on an animal patient. (As always when writing fiction, to respect the privacy of all humans and nonhumans, change details as necessary to protect their identities.)

Along these lines, try to write a little bit each day, even when you're deep into research. Even writing just a few lines of dialogue or half a scene helps keep you connected to the story—and it will also help you keep all the information relevant.

Finally, one benefit of writing while you're researching is that you'll be able to ask questions that are directly relevant to your story and/or characters. For example, if you've scheduled a ride-along with your local police department at the same time you're developing your characters and see a romantic subplot brewing, you might ask, "What would happen if a police officer sleeps with a suspect?" Not only will this help you with your novel, but people usually get a kick out of such writerly questions.

A style guide for writing for animals

Like most publishers, Ashland Creek Press uses such standard style guides as Merriam-Webster's dictionary and *The Chicago Manual of Style*—but we also have a few of our own "house rules," one of which is to give animals pronouns, i.e., not to use the word *it* to refer to an animal, unless the point of the dialogue or scene requires this.

If a character views animals as objects, for example, this character would use the term *it*. But in general, we find that a subtle but important way to advocate for animals is to use pronouns that eliminate the distance we normally place between human and nonhuman animals.

This brings up a few writerly questions, such as: How do we use *he* or *she* when we don't know the gender of the animal? If you're writing fiction, this is when you get to be creative. If credibility allows, you can simply make up the gender of the animal. If it's a bit trickier than that—as it was when Midge was writing both *Floreana* and *My Last Continent*—you have to stretch a bit. Midge wanted to be sure that the individual penguins readers met in these novels were given pronouns (if not actual names). In reality, guessing a penguin's gender at a glance can be challenging for even the most experienced of scientists—but all she had to do was make it credible for the reader by building their confidence in the naturalists' expertise and using good descriptions of the penguins.

Another option, if it's impossible to credibly gauge gender in a scene, is to simply use the gender-neutral pronoun *they*.

Pronouns matter, but if you have animal characters, whether major or minor to the story, it's important to give them names, if possible. Most companion animals, of course, are named in both real life and on the page, but don't shy away from naming all animals if you can. In both fiction and nonfiction, naming animals has a profound effect, as they become characters in their own right.

Scientists, wary of anthropomorphism, very rarely name the animals they study. Turbo the penguin was an exception.

We met Turbo in 2006 in Punta Tombo, Argentina, when we were volunteering with a penguin census at the Magellanic penguin colony there. Turbo, named by the scientists after the truck he tried to build his nest under, followed us around as he did all the researchers (who did not feed or otherwise encourage him), more like a pet than a wild animal. Having never chosen a mate (apparently the females weren't impressed with his truck as a proper nesting site), he was far more interested in humans—and getting to know him helped us see why he became a poster boy for the penguins of the world.

While penguins are generally either shy or too busy for humans, Turbo showed us his curiosity, his smarts, his good looks, and his fragile existence; the Center for Ecosystem Sentinels regularly sent out emails with news not only of the state of the colony but also the latest about Turbo. Getting to know one extraordinary bird helped the scientists at the Center give a face to the hundreds of thousands of penguins who need support.

Turbo also inspired our writing in immeasurable ways. John created a fictional penguin named Diesel in *The Tourist Trail* (obviously, he changed the name to protect Turbo's identity), and in *My Last Continent* Midge created a penguin character named Admiral Byrd, after the explorer. Our goals with these penguin characters were to be sure that readers could get to know them, as we got to know Turbo, and see that all of the millions of penguins struggling for survival in a changing climate are individuals.

We are not the only writers to name animals. Karen Joy Fowler's novel *We Are All Completely Beside Ourselves* features a nonhuman family member named Fern, who is seen no differently by the narrator from her human family members.

In *Barn 8*, Deb Olin Unferth introduces us to a chicken named Bwwaauk, who escapes from a cage and is found on the road by a human who ends up staging a rescue. Though *Barn 8* details the mass horrors of factory farming, meeting

Bwwaauk as an individual heightens the gravity of everything the chickens endure.

If it doesn't work for the narrative to give the animal a name, you might find another way to recognize this animal as an individual. In Charlotte McConaghy's novel *Once There Were Wolves*, the narrator, Inti, a biologist reintroducing wolves to the Scottish Highlands, resists naming the wolves to avoid growing attached, but she does get attached. While she names only one wolf in the story, the numbers by which they're called are as much like names in the affection and reverence she has for each animal.

Though she may know them seemingly impersonally as Number Eight or Number Ten, she also knows the color and striations of their fur, their personalities and habits. The names, in this case, matter less than Inti's reverence for them and her deep and profound knowledge of them.

If you're writing nonfiction, it may be impossible to give an animal a name. As one example, in her book about the dairy industry, *The Cow with Ear Tag #1389*, Kathryn Gillespie cannot name these individuals by anything other than their tags, but with this title she is still able to give a face to the 9.3 million dairy cows in the U.S. that are used for their milk until they are spent and sent to slaughter.

✎ WRITING PROMPT

- Write about your least favorite animal.
- Next, write about adopting and living with this animal.

- Pay close attention to pronouns, avoiding the use of *it*.

✐ WRITING PROMPT

- Write a scene, or choose a scene from your work in progress, that features an animal. Write the scene using *it* to refer to the animal.

- Next, change *it* to a pronoun.

- Finally, give the animal a name.

- Write about the differences between the scenes when you change from *it* to *he/she/they* to a name.

✐ WRITING PROMPT

- Write a scene featuring a human, or choose a scene from your work in progress, and change the pronoun to *it*.

- Write about how this affects the reader's view of the character.

Part 4:
Along the Way: Prompts & Inspiration

Always be writing

We always like to say there's no such thing as writer's block—because we have prompts!

Whenever you feel stuck—whether it's in the middle of a project or in the beginning as you're facing the blank page—these prompts are designed to help you. If you're feeling dejected—which is entirely possible when writing about difficult topics—these prompts will galvanize you back into action. If you're feeling uninspired, these prompts will remind you why you write what you write.

In this section you'll find myriad prompts for whatever place you're in. You may find that some prompts relate to your project; you may also choose a completely unrelated prompt (often, getting a bit of distance from a piece of writing is just the thing).

However you approach this section, it is here to accomplish one thing: to get you writing.

Inspired prompts

"To my mind, the life of a lamb is no less precious than that of a human being. The more helpless the creature, the more that it is entitled to protection by man from the cruelty of man." —Mahatma Gandhi

✐ WRITING PROMPT

- Write about an animal you fear or dislike (or used to), and give that animal a backstory. For example, if you're writing about a shark who feels predatory to you, write about her as a baby, including her interactions with family and how she now lives in the ocean. If you're writing about a cockroach, write about how this creature came to be in your kitchen and all that he's doing to survive.

✐ WRITING PROMPT

- Describe an animal who has been deprived of their freedom—for example, a hen or pig at a factory farm, a dog or cat at a shelter, a wild animal in a trap. Write a description of the animal based on observation only (physical details, behavior), and then write about the situation from the animal's point of view.

"To be alive and explore nature now is to read by the light of a library as it burns." —Tom Mustill

✎ WRITING PROMPT

- What animal do you feel is being studied and simultaneously endangered? This could be a species whose attention from scientists is doing them harm, for example, or an animal who needs to be better understood to be saved. Include a scene in which you write about how you got to know about this animal.

✎ WRITING PROMPT

- What animal would you bring back from extinction if you could, and why? Write about a day in the life of this animal, having been restored to their natural habitat. How does this change the world around them?

"Everyone is a genius. But if you judge a fish by its ability to climb a tree, it will live its whole life believing that it is stupid." —Albert Einstein

✎ WRITING PROMPT

- Think of an animal who is often perceived by humans as "stupid." What is the most genius thing about this animal?

- • Write about animals who have talents that humans do not have—for example, bats using echolocation, dogs' keen sense of smell, snails' ability to carry their homes around. Come up with as many examples as you can find, and then write a scene featuring one of these animals.

🌱

"The greatness of a nation can be judged by the way its animals are treated." —Mahatma Gandhi

✎ WRITING PROMPT

- • Write about an animal often viewed as a "pest"— from racoons to ants to roaches—as if they are revered. Create a world—it could be imaginative or fact-based, or a little of both—in which this animal is sacred, and why.

✎ WRITING PROMPT

- • Write about an animal who is revered in one culture but reviled in another. How does the treatment of animals vary across the world? What animal would you especially like to see treated better?

"I see that dogdom is in every way a marvelous institution." —Franz Kafka, "Investigations of a Dog"

✎ WRITING PROMPT

- What animal kingdom do you feel is a "marvelous institution"? Write from the point of view of one of these animals.

✎ WRITING PROMPT

- Imagine a companion animal who is not typical—instead of a housecat, for example, a house chicken; instead of a new puppy, a new baby goat. How does your perception of certain animals change when they are part of your everyday life rather than used for food?

"A man can live and be healthy without killing animals for food; therefore, if he eats meat, he participates in taking animal life merely for the sake of his appetite. And to act so is immoral." —Leo Tolstoy

✎ WRITING PROMPT

- If you eat animals or used to, write about an animal you have eaten, whether a chicken, pig, cow, or snails; if you are vegetarian and eat eggs and dairy, write about a chicken or a cow. Imagine a day in the life of this animal, in two different ways—in one scenario, she is being raised for food. In another, she is living at a sanctuary or in the natural world. Be as detailed as possible.

✎ WRITING PROMPT

- Think of something you feel is immoral—for example, lying or stealing—and write a scene in which a character does just that, with no qualms whatsoever. How do the people around this character react? Do they accept the behavior? Do they confront the character? Do they embrace the behavior themselves? Write all that you can, and see where this takes you.

❧

"Nothing will benefit health and increase the chances for survival of life on earth as the evolution of a vegetarian diet." —Albert Einstein

✎ WRITING PROMPT

> **Part 1:** Consider the region in which you live, and write about your experience of animal agriculture in your area, whether it's 4-H, an industrial pig farm, a processing plant, a small family farm, or even backyard chickens. If you don't live near any farming practices, take a day trip and see what you find. How does this area differ from where you live—visually, geographically, economically?
>
> **Part 2:** Next, envision what the region might look like if no animals are being raised or processed for food in your state, province, or country. How would the landscape change? How would the humans adapt? How would you feel about it?

✎ WRITING PROMPT

- Visit an animal rights website, and look at photos and videos of animal agriculture (this will not be easy). Then, visit a sanctuary website and look at the photos and videos of rescued animals. Write about the details of what you've seen, focusing on physical details and sounds. Then write about what you perceive the animals were feeling (from the expressions in their eyes, on their faces, in how they move).

"When novelists attempt to write from the point of view of a nonhuman animal, they are accused of illegitimate anthropomorphism. Sometimes criticism of some sort is due, if the novelist has not bothered to investigate the life-world of that type of creature, but has lazily imagined the animal as rather like a human in a costume." —Martha C. Nussbaum, *Justice for Animals: Our Collective Responsibility*

✐ WRITING PROMPT

- Write about the depiction of an animal in fiction that you felt was all wrong.

- Next, write about how you'd do it differently.

✐ WRITING PROMPT

- Choose an animal about which you know very little—an insect you've never seen in real life, for example, or a wild animal you've never encountered. Next, research this animal and learn as much as you can about their life—everything from where they live to what they eat to how they mate. (Note: Use every resource you can, from books and journals to documentaries and nature videos.) Finally, write a scene featuring this animal, using all that you've learned.

Timed prompts & lists

✎ WRITING PROMPT

- Write about the best ten things about your companion animal.

- Write about the ten most annoying things about your companion animal.

✎ WRITING PROMPT

- Write about your favorite animal in 100 words or fewer.

✎ WRITING PROMPT

Part 1: Set a timer for five minutes. Write a list of all the animals you'd love to see in the wild, wherever in the world they might be.

Part 2: Next, set a timer for ten minutes and rework your list to categorize the animals who live in the same regions—for example, wombats and kangaroos in Australia, or bears and bald eagles in Alaska.

Part 3: Finally, set a timer for fifteen minutes and write down all that you know of these animals and why you're intrigued by them; include physical description, their habitat, what traits they have that you admire, and so on.

Using the senses

✎ WRITING PROMPT

- Write about an animal using only the sense of sound.

- Write about an animal using only the sense of sight.

- Write about an animal using only the sense of touch.

- Write about an animal using only the sense of taste (i.e, the animal's sense of taste).

- Write about an animal using only the sense of smell.

- Write about an animal using only the sixth sense— how the animal makes you feel.

✎ WRITING PROMPT

- Go for a walk. Find a place to stop where you can observe an animal—a duck in a pond, a snake on a trail, a bird in a tree. Write down everything you can about this animal, based on your observations only: sights, sounds, smells. Next, write down what you imagine this animal may be thinking based on his or her behavior.

✎ WRITING PROMPT

- Write about the sound of your companion animal eating.

- Write about the sound of your companion animal sleeping.

✐ WRITING PROMPT

- Listen to the sounds of animals around you, whether you're at home or walking in your neighborhood. When a neighbor's dog barks, what do you think he is saying? When a crow screeches overhead, what do you think she's trying to say? Imagine what various animals are trying to communicate—to humans and to one another.

✐ WRITING PROMPT

- Write about an animal smell that you love. Write about one you dislike.

✐ WRITING PROMPT

- Write about the texture of an animal, whether a chicken or a goat or a cat.

✐ WRITING PROMPT

- Write about something you may never touch—such as a bear's claws or a lion's tongue—and what this might look and feel like, up close.

Animals among us

In 1457, French villagers took a sow and six piglets to court for attacking and killing a five-year-old boy. The sow was sentenced to be hanged; the piglets were exonerated.

In 1621 in Germany, a cow knocked over a woman, who later died of her injuries. The cow was put on trial and sentenced to death.

In 1659 in Italy, caterpillars were charged with trespassing in the gardens, fields, and orchards and damaging the plants. It appears that the court recognized the caterpillars' right to life, liberty, and the pursuit of happiness, but the ultimate decision remains unknown.

✐ **WRITING PROMPT**

- What animal(s) would you put on trial if you could, and for what offense?

- What animal(s) would you defend at trial?

Peter Benchley's novel *Jaws* (as well as the film based on the book) led to an unrealistic, unwarranted, and nearly universal fear of sharks.

Ranchers in the West are beginning to work with beavers rather than against them—instead of blowing up their dams, they are welcoming the beavers' work, which helps restore and enhance their properties.

- What animal(s) have seen a changed human perception about them in your lifetime?

- What animal(s) did you grow up fearing or disliking whom you now like, respect, and/or admire?

Consider the following:

Asian giant hornets are often called "murder hornets."

Orcas are called "killer whales."

The mosquito is the most dangerous animal in the world (malaria); humans are second (homicides).

✐ WRITING PROMPT

- What animal has a scary name or nickname that is not at all dangerous to humans?

- What animal do you fear the most, and why?

- How does the name of an animal affect your perception of them?

Consider the following:

To hunt, the fringed jumping spider can make herself look like forest detritus caught in a web by changing coloring and vibrating in her web to attract her prey.

Zebras are striped to make it hard for predators to pick out an individual in a crowd.

Plovers fake broken wings to draw predators away from their nests.

✐ WRITING PROMPT

> **Part 1:** What superpower would you like to have to help you navigate your own human life—e.g., in what situations would you like to be able to disappear, or blend in, or elude an unwelcome person? Think like a nonhuman animal to choose your superpower— but write it from a human perspective.
>
> **Part 2:** Next, write about an animal you know or have observed (a companion animal, a neighborhood squirrel, the mice in your garage) and write about a superpower they have—i.e., what talents do they have that enable them to survive and thrive?

Let's chat

✐ WRITING PROMPT

- Pick two animals who may appear to be natural enemies—for example, predator and prey such as a lion and a gazelle, or two tomcats encountering each other in an alley. Write a dialogue between them. What would they say to each other?

✐ WRITING PROMPT

- Write a dialogue between two of your companion animals. It could be between the two of your cats who snuggle together, or the two who don't seem to get along. It could be between your dog and your goldfishes, or the two companion rabbits you're trying to bond.

✐ WRITING PROMPT

Part 1: Write a conversation you would like to have with one of your companion animals. What do you imagine each of you would say?

Part 2: Next, write a conversation between you and an animal you have eaten/worn/ridden/seen at a zoo or aquarium. What do you imagine each of you would say?

Part 3: Finally, write a conversation between you and a wild animal you encountered recently, whether a bear on a hike or a racoon in your trash bin. What do you imagine each of you would say?

✎ WRITING PROMPT

- Write a letter to someone, human or animal. Some suggestions are below.
    - ° Dear Animal Activist
    - ° Dear Carnivore
    - ° Dear Vegan
    - ° Dear Farmer
    - ° Dear Cow
    - ° Dear Chicken
    - ° Dear Calf
    - ° Dear Pig

✎ WRITING PROMPT

- Write an apology to an animal. You might start with a domestic animal (telling your cat you're sorry you didn't feed her at 2 a.m. as she requested), and go on to apologize to a species you don't know very well. Try apologizing to farm animals, to insects, to endangered species.

Imagine

✐ WRITING PROMPT

- If you could live a life as a nonhuman animal, which animal would you choose and why? Write about a day in your life as this animal.

✐ WRITING PROMPT

- Find a lost-pet poster in your area, or look at a description of one online (if you search "lost pets," you'll find many in your area). Write about this pet's time apart from their family—and conclude with them being adopted by a new family, or reunited with their original family.

✐ WRITING PROMPT

- Write a scene from the point of view of an animal whose experience of the world is vastly different from ours as humans—for example, bats, or whales, or bees.

✐ WRITING PROMPT

- Write about an animal who is misunderstood (and perhaps neglected, abused, or endangered) because of human limitations. How might we humans do better to understand this animal?

✎ WRITING PROMPT

• An octopus expresses fear or anger by changing color. In what nonverbal ways do you yourself express fear and/or anger? In what ways do the animals you observe (your companion animals, local birds, wildlife) express fear and/or anger? What other emotions do you see animals expressing with their behaviors?

✎ WRITING PROMPT

• Write an obituary for an animal—it could be a pet, a famous animal, a wild animal. It could be a mouse who was caught in a trap, a squirrel who got hit by a car, a bug who got underfoot on a sidewalk. Write it in the style of a newspaper obituary.

✎ WRITING PROMPT

• Many birds mate for life, while others are wildly promiscuous. Write a scene in which any bird, from a swan to a penguin to a hummingbird, discovers his or her partner has been cheating with another bird.

✎ WRITING PROMPT

• Think about an animal whom many might consider a pest (rabbits in a garden, cockroaches in a kitchen, ants on the porch, and so on), and write a scene (or a story, or a poem) that celebrates this "pesky" animal.

✎ WRITING PROMPT

Part 1: Pick a group of people (e.g., your family, colleagues, friends) and turn them all into a group of animals (farm animals, an endangered species, companion animals). Write a scene featuring all of them as this new species.

Part 2: Next, choose an animal (a wild animal, your companion animal, an urban animal like a rat or pigeon) and turn this individual into a human animal. Write a scene in which they go about their day in this new physical form.

✎ WRITING PROMPT

- Think of an animal endemic to a certain place—polar bears of the Arctic, for example, or tortoises of the Galápagos—and give this animal a passport. Imagine the animal traveling to a faraway place, and write a scene, story, or poem about their adventures.

Part 5:
Paths to Publication

Publishing for animals

There are a great many books and resources about publishing, so we won't go into too much detail here about general publishing. But we do want to mention a few things about publishing for animals specifically.

When it comes to animal rights, the world is still catching up. Few mainstream publishers are releasing novels about animal rights; while animal memoirs are reader-friendly and popular, books about animal abuse are challenging. And if publishers fear the audience isn't there, they're not likely to back such books. This is the reason Ashland Creek Press came into being in 2011; we saw very few opportunities for environmental and animal writing, so we created our own.

Fortunately, the world is already changing—and the opportunities will only become greater. But you'll need to be patient, as all writers must be.

If you're not already familiar with EcoLit Books, this is a great online source for environmental and animal literature. In addition to book reviews, you'll also find myriad opportunities for writers, from literary magazines and journals to publishers open to environmental work.

Find your path

In many ways, this is the golden age of publishing. More than a hundred thousand books are published every year, in myriad ways—from self-publishing to hybrid publishing to traditional publishing.

And because there are so many options, it's important to invest the time in understanding how publishing works—in all its incarnations—so that you can make an informed decision.

First, a little historical context.

The merging of large corporations has led to a great deal of consolidation in publishing. As of this writing, there are five major publishers—Hachette Book Group, HarperCollins, Macmillan, Penguin Random House, and Simon & Schuster—known as the Big Five. To publish within one of the dozens of imprints of the Big Five, you need a literary agent.

There are also dozens of small and university presses that do not fall under the Big Five, and for many of these smaller publishers, you can approach editors directly. While you may not get as large an advance or publicity budget, there are a great many advantages of going with a smaller press, such as closer attention to your work and more accessible staff.

Finally, many smaller presses are not traditional publishers but hybrid publishers—and this is an important distinction. Read on to learn more.

Traditional publishing

In the traditional publishing model, the publisher pays the author an advance, and then it pays royalties once the author has earned out the advance. For example, if you get an advance of $10,000, you will receive royalties (a percentage of sales) on books sold only after you've earned back this advance. With the smaller presses, authors may not receive advances, but in that case they will begin receiving royalties right away. Authors pay nothing to the publisher under the traditional publishing model.

Because in this traditional model the publisher takes all the financial risk, the publisher will also be in charge of all aspects of publication. For example, many authors with large publishers don't have a say in what their book cover will look like—this isn't always the case, but it's something to be prepared for. And while traditional publishers take on the costs of production (everything from editorial to printing) as well as marketing and promotion, they often put most of their resources toward big-name authors—so do be prepared to handle much of your own book promotion. That said, with a large publisher, you'll have the advantage of solid distribution and a large team of industry professionals.

With a smaller traditional publisher, you will still be paid for your work, and you'll have the advantage of working much more closely with a smaller team. Also, because small presses take on fewer books a year, the time they'll be able to devote to your book is greater than a large publisher, which must move on to the next season's books fairly quickly.

Self-publishing

If you self-publish, you'll need a budget because the self-published author pays for everything. Depending on your skills and expertise, you may need to pay for editing, proofreading, book design, book cover design, e-books, audiobooks, a website, and marketing expenses, among other costs.

On the plus side, though you'll likely be investing a lot up front, you get to keep all the proceeds from your book sales (minus the percentages from online retailers).

As a self-published author, you'll also have to manage promotion on your own (unless you have a budget to hire a book marketing professional). Ideally, a self-published author is a self-starter with an entrepreneurial spirit, a strong platform, a healthy budget, and a lively social media presence.

Hybrid publishing

"Hybrid" publishing has evolved as a cross between traditional and self-publishing. With the hybrid model, a publisher will charge the author for everything but then do all the work. So, with a hybrid publisher, your book may receive whatever editing and design services you pay for—from copyediting and proofreading to marketing—depending on the publishing package and how much you spend. You'll also probably have to pay for the printing of your own books.

This model is fine for those who don't have the skills necessary to self-publish or who prefer to have a team working for them. But this is the key to hybrid publishing—you are a client more than an author. Whereas a traditional publisher pays for all aspects of publishing your book and therefore works hard to sell it, a hybrid press makes its money from you, the author, for its services, and it doesn't matter to them whether your book sells.

Whether you are traditionally published or self-published, you are the best salesperson for your book. When your book is published, the journey is really just beginning. You'll need to be prepared to do social media promotion; events, in-person and/or virtual; additional (often unpaid) writing, such as book reviews, op-eds, articles, and essays; and anything else that might help get your book in front of readers.

A few resources

Below are a few resources we recommend for familiarizing yourself with the publishing world and learning as much as you can before you venture into it.

- Publishers Weekly (www.publishersweekly.com)
- Poets & Writers (www.pw.org)
- Publisher's Marketplace (www. publishersmarketplace.com)

These three resources have free newsletters you can subscribe to, as well as paid access to a wealth of additional information.

We also recommend following longtime publishing guru Jane Friedman (www.JaneFriedman.com), whose blog offers insights and advice in all aspects of publishing.

One of the best things you can do not only for your book but for your sanity as a writer is to connect with other writers. You can do this through writing communities (many of which have robust online programs, due to the pandemic), such as San Diego Writers, Ink (San Diego), GrubStreet Writers (Boston), Hugo House (Seattle), or The Loft (Minneapolis).

Environmental and animal conferences are also great places to meet like-minded souls, such as the Animal Rights National Conference (www.arconference.org), the Association for the

Study of Literature and the Environment, or ASLE (www. asle.org), and Minding Animals (www.mindinganimals.com).

✎ WRITING PROMPT
- Write about your goal for the piece you are currently working on. Where do you envision it being published?
- Make a list of ten places to send it, whether to literary agents or publishers, literary magazines or newspapers.

✎ WRITING PROMPT
- Make a list of things you'd like to know about publishing, from editing to book promotion.
- Check out online resources to see where you might be able to take a class, attend a conference, or join a group to learn more.

✎ WRITING PROMPT
- Write down the things you struggle with most as a writer—for example, getting started, writing dialogue, or revision.
- Write down any connections you have with the idea of forming a writers' group. For example: fellow writers from a class you took, writers in a membership organization who write in the same genre, or like-minded colleagues.

On rejection & criticism

"It is difficult to get a man to understand something, when his salary depends upon his not understanding it." —Upton Sinclair

Rejection is part of the process of being a writer—and especially of being a literary activist. Much of the world may not be quite ready to hear the truths you're writing about; the ways our society uses and abuses animals makes readers (including agents and editors) uncomfortable, and when your animal writing is rejected, you should know that this is not necessarily due to the quality of your work but a (conscious or even subconscious) reaction to the material. Likewise, even when you do get published, you may find reader reactions (including book reviews) to be similarly difficult.

How to deal with rejection

The first thing we tell ourselves is that when one agent, editor, or publication rejects us, the door opens to another agent, editor, or publication. Then we turn our attention to what's next on our list. By focusing on the future and not the past, you will be in a better mental state. Most important is to never (ever) give up. You're not alone—and the more of us who write for animals, the more the world will read and change. The animals need us.

On editing and compromise

Even when your work gets accepted for publication, you still need to be prepared for input and suggestions you might not agree with.

The more mainstream the media outlet, the more likely you will get feedback along the lines of: "Can you soften this?" Or "Does this character really need to be vegan?" Before you push back, take a deep breath. Mainstream media is mainstream for a reason—it wants to appeal to as many people as possible. And, as a writer hoping to open hearts and minds, this is your goal as well. So anything that editors feel might be off-putting to readers will become points for discussion.

But remember: If they've accepted your work, they are already invested in what you're presenting. Editing is often a two-way street, which means you can find common ground.

Also, take time to consider what you're willing to give up to get your work into the world. Maybe a few tweaks will still get the message out, albeit slightly watered down. Ask yourself: Is this better than not getting the work out into the world at all? The larger the audience, the greater opportunity for impact on a large scale.

Criticism is not easy to take, for most of us. It can hurt, and it can feel personal, particularly if it's about animal rights or veganism—issues central to who we are. But always keep in mind that your editor may not have similar views. Stay focused on the end goal—getting your animal writing into the world.

If, however, you refuse to make any changes, refuse to take any vegan message out, that's your prerogative. But do be prepared for more pushback from mainstream outlets. On the other hand, you may have more opportunities from progressive outlets.

Ultimately, you have to listen to your gut. Where would you be most proud to see your work? Start there.

✏ WRITING PROMPT

- Consider a piece you have ready for submission, whether it's a novel to send to agents or a poem to send to journals.

- Write a detailed rejection letter to yourself, staying focused on the writing and the content.

- Next, write a detailed acceptance letter to yourself, again staying focused on the writing and the content.

Publication is just the beginning

To see your story, essay, poem, or book out in the world is an amazing feeling. Enjoy it.

Then remember that publication is not the end—it is the beginning.

Promotion is the next and never-ending step of living the writing life, particularly if you've published a book. Your publisher will want you to promote it in every way possible, and if you're self-published or hybrid published, you'll want to do the same.

With the numerous (and seemingly endless) ways to promote your work—and an abundance of books and blogs about this topic—we won't go into all the details here. But, as with your writing, consider your audience when promoting your animal-themed work. You'll want to focus on animal-receptive audiences—as well as those who may want to learn something new. If you've written in a specific genre, target those readers, as well as those who may love the species included in your book.

Most of all, keep in mind that it can be a challenge, with so many distractions in the world, to find readers—so be patient, be persistent, and keep at it. Your work will be brand-new to anyone who hasn't read it yet, so even as you embark on your next writing project, always be thinking of how to keep getting the word out about what you've already published.

The animal hero's journey

It took Odysseus ten years to make it home from the fields of Troy, a journey that gave us one of the great works of literature. While we hope your journey to publication is less arduous and far faster, do remember to appreciate the journey, perhaps even enjoy it.

As writers, we naturally focus our energies on seeing our work all the way to publication. But publication should not be viewed only as the destination but as another stop along your lifetime journey as a writer. Everything we write—published or unpublished—is part of that journey.

More important, it's critical that you not view publication as the arbiter of success or failure. Rejection is an inevitable part of being a writer. Many of the world's most successful writers—from Stephen King to Ursula K. Le Guin to Madeleine L'Engle—were rejected dozens of times before finding success. And not everything you write may find a publisher, but if you keep at it, your best work will. The only certainty is that if you give up, you won't succeed—so don't give up!

This journey you are on is not an easy one. But it is also one of the most important journeys a writer can undertake—turning your passion into action, and changing the world one word at a time.

We wish you the absolute best on your journey. And remember that we're all just getting started in writing for animals. The world will catch up with us.

—Midge & John

About Midge Raymond

Midge Raymond is the author of the novels *Floreana* and *My Last Continent* and the award-winning short-story collection *Forgetting English*. Her writing has appeared in *TriQuarterly*, *American Literary Review*, *Bellevue Literary Review*, the *Los Angeles Times*, the *Chicago Tribune, Poets & Writers*, and other publications. She has taught writing at Boston University and at Boston's GrubStreet Writers; Seattle's Richard Hugo House; San Diego Writers, Ink; and at writing conferences around the world.

About John Yunker

John Yunker is the author of the novels *The Tourist Trail* and *Where Oceans Hide Their Dead*. He is editor of the *Among Animals* fiction series and the nonfiction anthology *Writing for Animals*. His plays have been produced or staged at such venues as the Oregon Contemporary Theatre, the Source Festival, the Centre Stage New Play Festival, and the Association for Theatre in Higher Education conference. His teleplay *Sanctuary* was performed at the Compassion Arts Festival in New York, and his short stories have been published in *Phoebe, Qu, Flyway, Antennae,* and other journals.

Ashland Creek Press is an independent, vegan-owned publisher of eco-literature, which includes books in all genres about animals, the environment, and the planet we all call home. We are passionate about books that foster an appreciation for worlds outside our own, for nature and the animal kingdom, and for the ways in which we all connect. To keep up to date on new and forthcoming works, subscribe to our newsletter at www.AshlandCreekPress.com.

* 9 7 8 1 6 1 8 2 2 1 0 3 2 *